HIJACKED BY

Be Afraid: Be Very, Very Afraid

I0014601

By Michael Klein

Table of Contents

INTRODUCTION: PROFILE OF A HACKER

Most of us have this stereotypical idea of what a hacker looks like or what they act like, but today's hackers have evolved into a whole new breed. They are no longer the geeky guy in the office or the introverted high school teenager who messes with computers because he has no social life. If that's still your picture, you've got some ugly surprises coming your way. Today's hackers are hidden to us; they exist in society's shadows, living in an underworld subculture.

Many are not motivated by greed or social acceptance. Instead, they live to create chaos and to convince sociopathic followers of their discovery. It's a beautiful thing they believed they have learned, and now they're enlightened. What they believe is that there is beauty in darkness, comfort in chaos, and hidden power in hijacking the lives of others. In reality, hackers are controlled by the cowardly act of hacking.

Today's hackers are not playing the rather innocent games of curious, intelligent teens. No! They are out to destroy, and you could be their next target.

To demonstrate how dangerous this dark art of hacking can be, let me tell you a story about a man who tried to break into the infamous group of hackers known as LulzSec.

Story of Aaron Barr and the LulzSec Hackers

Aaron Barr was an ambitious CEO of a security software company known as HBGary Federal. His business had been struggling to make a name for itself in the security industry, so Barr originated an idea that he believed would give him extensive publicity and significantly increase his client base. He and his team would use all their security know-how and technological savvy to reveal the identities of an infamous hacking group called LulzSec.

Knowing that a hacker's greatest fear is for his/her true identity to be revealed, Barr thought he was prepared for the onslaught. As it turned out, his early estimation of the group's leaders consisting of a band of intelligent and highly curious teens who had too much time on their hands was a dangerously false assumption. His folly of trying to expose the group came at a higher price than he could have ever imagined.

The core members of LulzSec were sophisticated hackers whose purpose was to destroy and wreak havoc on any entity or person who challenged their secret activities. The cost of Barr's investigations to uncover their identities and reveal their whereabouts resulted in the seizure of his Facebook, Twitter, Yahoo, and Warcraft accounts. LulzSec replaced Barr's homepage with a posted message. Part of this message is as follows:

"...You've clearly overlooked something very obvious here: we are everyone

and we are no one. If you swing a sword of malice into our innards, we

will simply engulf it. You cannot break us, you cannot harm us, even

though you have clearly tried..."

LulzSec also put a link to HBGary's Security Federal's homepage that contained 50,000 private corporate emails revealing information that was obviously never meant to be seen by the public. Barr's CTO owned a separate company with its website of 80,000 registered members, and that too was obliterated.

To Barr's surprise and his company's demise, at the core of the LutzSec hackers were a handful of criminally minded activists whose ambitions were to be what they considered the world's superheroes. Whenever they perceived injustice, they would man their stations on the Internet and avenge the imagined harm. Of course, LutzSec was judge and jury, vigilantes on a worldwide scale.

Its leaders ranged from the ages of 16 to 28 years old, with an arsenal of computer power and genius operators who had the knowledge and specialized skills to impact history. After being introduced to this group, you'll have a more accurate profile of today's hackers.

Jake Davis (alias Topiary) was 18 years old when he was arrested for his activities in LulzSec. Jake was the spokesperson for the group—not the most technologically skilled but by far the most articulate. Whenever there were victims to be taunted and haunting threats used to appease LulzSec's fans, Jake was front-row-center. Jake authored many messages designed to debase his imagined enemies and entertain his followers.

When the police finally caught up with Jake at his home on the Shetland Islands, they found 17 virtual machines running on an encrypted drive. His last infamous message on Twitter before his arrest was *"You cannot arrest an idea."*

Next, there is Mustafa Al-Bassam (alias Tflow). Tflow was just 16 years old when he was arrested in London, England. He was the groups highly skilled coder. Although Tflow was quite socially awkward in person, his online persona was just the opposite. Because of his calm and collected online poise, Tflow was believed to be much older than he was. When asked, one of the group's members thought him to be at least 30 years old. However, Tflow's young age did not stop him from planning such sophisticated hacks that they would change the face of an entire nation.

It was Tflow who wrote such advanced code that allowed citizens of Tunisia to get past their government's ISP restrictions during the Arab Spring and post on social media. Through Tflow's incredible coding skills, an entire nation of people was empowered.

We cannot forget to mention Ryan Ackroyd (alias Kayla), from Yorkshire, England. He was one of the older hackers in the group—24 years old at the time of his arrest. As a teen, Ryan formed a group that played a lot of video games. It was somewhat like a virtual gang, with Ryan as the ringleader. On one occasion, a rival virtual gang hacked into Ryan's group and targeted one of their youngest members—Kayla. Kayla had been welcomed into the group by Ryan, and he had grown quite fond of their online friendship.

The rival hacker gang viciously destroyed Kayla's social networks, even breaking into her parent's back account. Out for revenge, Ryan fought back, honoring Kayla by using her name as his alias. His revengeful retribution was so devastating that Kayla has the reputation on the Internet as being a force you want as an ally—not an enemy. It was Kayla who was responsible for engineering her way into Barr's CTO's company's website and simply deleting all its data. It was Kayla who discovered SQL injection insecurity on the HBGary Federal website. It was also Kayla who later developed and wrote a program to scan URLs many times per second looking for zero days.

To show you how invasive zero days are, let me explain what they are. Zero days are undisclosed computer software vulnerabilities that hackers use to negatively impact programs, data, and networks. It's called zero days because you never know it's happened until there is zero time to react.

Kayla, or Ryan, was self-taught and the most skilled hacker of the group. His role was to provide server penetration, and there was rarely a server he couldn't crack. When he was arrested, his apartment was trip-wired so that as the police entered all the computer hard drives would be wiped out. Certainly, the youthful, innocent, geeky kind of image we have of a hacker is not in evidence in Ryan Ackroyd.

Lastly, we have Hector Monsegur (alias Sabu) from New York City. Sabu was one of the oldest leaders of LulzSec; he was 28 years old at the time of his arrest. Sabu was the commander of the group, driving the daily operations and settling the squabbles between its members.

Sabu's background and purposes were much different than others in LulzSec. He was what is known as an "hactivist," which is one who believes in hacking for a greater political or social cause. From Puerto Rico, Sabu was the first to be identified by Barr. When the FBI confronted Sabu and promised him 100 plus years in federal prison, he quickly turned informant (1). I guess there is no loyalty among thieves.

I tell you this story to help you to realize the truth of the statement made by these hackers when they wrote: "...*we are everyone, and we are no one.*" Look around you; dangerous hackers sit beside you on the bus, eat at a nearby table in the restaurant, and party with your high schoolers. What they have in common is their ability and desire to devastate on a personal as well as a global level. Are you ready to take another look at the characteristics and personality traits that create the profile of a hacker? Good, let's analyze the data that has been collected on many sociopathic hackers.

Character Traits of a Hacker

Some of the most important and distinct character traits of hackers are their high intelligence, curiosity, and countercultural behaviors and beliefs. Hackers are the epitome of nonconformists and are usually quite verbal about it—online of course. In person, you will rarely hear a word from them, as they are not gregarious by nature. The hacker will be the one standing alone in the corner of a room filled with hundreds of partiers. Because they care very little about impressing with their GQ appearance, they often look almost slovenly. What hackers value most are their minds, their ability to rise to the challenge of figuring out a puzzle or contemplating how to resolve troubling issues that others accept as normal.

In their youth, many hackers were attracted to toys and nifty gadgets they had to work out or solve. As children, they often isolated themselves from the innocent games kids play, preferring the more introverted games that allowed them to stand apart from their friends. The hacker's desire is to impress by thinking his or her way to a win. As children, they may have enjoyed the types of games where they alone manipulated and controlled the outcome. The game was not won by the role of a dice, but because of the strategies they employed.

As adults, hackers continue to cherish their ability to control the game of life—theirs and others. Looking at a hacker's work, you'll see very orderly and tidy code. Their workspace is a different matter, though. Those same kids that looked unkempt are the hackers with desks covered in magazines, papers, and dirty dishes with partially eaten sandwiches from days past. Uncaring of their immediate environment, hackers' reality is made up of the lives of many—including yours.

Since hackers maintain countercultural values, many live in communal settings. With their attention taken up 24/7 on or about their computers, their relationships are mostly virtual. Virtual connections are more desirable, making it unnecessary for them to struggle through the day-to-day challenges of a real-world relationship. In the real world, hackers would have to give up precious computer time to be attentive to the needs of others. Obviously, hackers' narcissistic tendencies prohibit most relationships that could positively influence their lives. A hacker's life is a lonely existence. What most of us fail to understand is that's the way they like it.

A List of Hackers' Common Character Traits and Behaviors

Although not all of these traits are predominant in hackers, many can be seen as common issues. Hackers most usually . . .

- Find it difficult to identify emotionally with others.
- Are sexually frustrated and socially withdrawn.
- Have plenty of time on their hands—either they are unemployed or spend a great deal of time alone.
- Drive cars that are filthy heaps in need of numerous repairs.
- Have cats for pets rather than dogs. Cats have that hacker mentality.
- Have stacks of unpaid bills on their desks.
- Defer household repairs until items are beyond fixing.
- Feel superior to others, especially those "idiots" who know nothing about computers.
- Impatient with tasks that waste their computer time.

- Are self-absorbed and intellectually arrogant.
- Cannot confront others face-to-face but can rip them apart with the use of technology.
- Are control freaks. They feel trapped by real-world relationships where they cannot close the screen when things get dicey.
- Not very motivated by social approval or even money.
- Have excellent memories and care most about rather obscure ideas and topics that most people find tedious to talk about (2).

If the hackers you've been introduced to in this book seem far too professional to be even remotely interested in breaking into your personal at-home computer, think again. They all began their careers as young children. They were hacking others, much like yourself, at an early age, honing their skills by breaking into the private emails and bank accounts of unsuspecting citizens. At first, they may not have done anything sinister. They were just little voyeurs, peeping into the lives of their neighbors, employers, or Facebook friends.

Then these annoying but rather innocent hackers began to evolve. In a matter of a few short years, they transformed into the dangerous criminals about whom you just read. Even though these professionals may not be interested in you individually, they do like the challenge of hacking huge corporations like Wal-mart, J.P. Morgan/Chase Bank, and even the IRS. Think about it! Every bit of information you provide to the IRS could be right now in the hands of a professional hacker.

The entire hacking industry, and believe me it is an industry, is evolving as much as the hackers themselves. What used to be hackers whose concerns were to make others suffer loss, now have learned that hacking can give them financial independence. Hacking is turning into big business, where backyard hackers are significantly impacting thousands of people's livelihoods.

Just yesterday in the news there was a small business owner in my hometown whose website was hacked. One simple little hack by a skilled expert that has cost her thousands of dollars in lost revenue. The hacker broke into her business website and placed the words "permanently closed" on her home page. They weren't big letters written across the page in a way that might signal the public that a hacker had been up to no good. No! They were placed in the top right corner as if added by the owner to let her customers know she had closed the business. In fact, it was only after several clients called to question her about why she had closed her business that she noticed those two little words "permanently closed" on her homepage.

The owner tried to get a friend to help her remove the message from her website, but to no avail. A few days later, the owner received a phone call on her business line stating that they would be happy to remove the words "permanently closed" from her website for $395. At first, she refused, knowing that she was being hijacked by a hacker. However, after searching several services to remove the coding, she discovered that it would be so challenging and the charges so astronomical that it was less expensive to pay the hackers to remove the coding. Closing down the website wasn't an option because all her clients' information was held in a database that the hackers also threatened to remove if the fee wasn't paid. To this day, the words "permanently closed" are on her website with a message beneath that reads, *"We're open—we were just hacked and can't remove the message."*

Something as simple as hacking photos off your Facebook page generated a lot of fear for one couple. Recently, there was a couple on the Dr. Phil show who were the proud parents of twins. Throughout the years, they had chronicled the lives of their children as they grew into beautiful little toddlers. One day, some friends of theirs reported a strange discovery. They saw pictures of the twins on another person's website.

As it turned out, for years this woman had been hacking the photos off the website and putting them on her own. She claimed they were her children, and even used Photoshop to remove the real mom from the pictures and add herself. When police investigated the story, they found photos of the twins proudly displayed in the stranger's home. Not only had she hacked their Facebook page, but she had hacked their children as well. The birth mother said she now lives in fear of this stranger who claimed her twins as her own.

The Internet has turned our world into a small place, capable of delivering an immense amount of information at the touch of a finger. In some respect that is a great thing, and in others it is a threat to the very fabric of our existence. It has made men and women who would otherwise have been petty criminals in their neighborhoods or cities, now be able to infect the Internet and spread their poisonous beliefs and behaviors on a global scale. Just look at the members of the LulzSec hackers. Their members consisted of thousands of hackers from around the world.

Just because you've never been unfortunate enough to be hacked, don't think their activities haven't affected you and your family. Every time a major corporation has to install added security, who do you think will cover those costs in the long run by higher prices of goods and services? Every time a school has to expel a young teen because they hacked into a teacher's computer, what do you think that teenage will do at home with all that time on their hands? Right! They'll be perfecting their hacking skills at your expense.

Some businesses benefit from hackers. There is a myriad of computer service companies who provide service contracts to sweep your computers and clean up any viruses that may have been the job of a former hacker. They may not have been involved in the hack, but they're still benefiting. Just like the website message mentioned earlier, some cause the problem and then offer to help you solve it. Most are not quite so obvious about their scandalous behaviors, but they're still after the payoff.

All this is what motivated us to write this book, to give you a glimpse of the people behind the mask of a hacker and to keep you abreast of what steps you can take to protect yourself. You'll learn how to identify a hacker and what to do if you suspect you've been hacked. All the information in this book will empower you as you learn how to avoid becoming the hacker's next victim.

With all the preventative measures and knowledge, there are some hackers so good that the only residue left is a random email or a slightly slower computer. When avoiding the hacker is impossible, it's good to have the assurance a backup plan provides. We'll be discussing those in a later chapter. It's all about refusing to be a victim. There are measures you can take that discourage or delay a hack attack, and implementation doesn't have to be pricey or complicated.

Congratulate yourself! You're taking the first step to protecting yourself against hackers who justify lurking in your private life because they have appointed themselves as worldwide watchdogs. The precautions we'll be telling you about work against the backyard hackers. If it's a die-hard professional, chances are you're going to be hacked. However, if a backyard hacker is targeting you, and they run up against quite a few delays trying to break into your personal or business computers or phones, they'll most likely move on to the next unprotected site.

Any delay for a hacker who perceives more wasted time than reward will hopefully be discouraged long enough for you to prevent financial or data loss from breached machines. The cunningness and creativity of many hackers, even the backyard variety, is eye-opening. You have to wonder what they could achieve if all that energy were channeled into something promising—something that would change our lives for the better, right?

Unfortunately, hackers are here to stay. What we can do is help you from being hijacked by a hacker. You deserve a right to privacy. When your privacy is compromised, you need to have a weapon to fight back. That weapon is knowledge. Knowing how to recognize you've been attacked and what to do afterward is crucial, but knowing how to fight back is empowering. Join us on our journey as we travel through the dark alleys of a hacker's mind. Discovering the hacker's beliefs and behaviors will provide insight into just where the next attack may occur. It could be within your home.

Chapter 1: It Could Happen to You

If you think you couldn't be hacked, you're living in a fool's world. Believe me, if hackers can break into government systems, phish major corporations' databases, and access U.S. military documents, your personal home computer is a piece of cake. Oh, I can hear you now! You're probably saying to yourself: *"Who would want to hack my computer? There's nothing of value they could get from me."* Wrong! They want information, and you have stored information on your computer. Let me ask you—do you pay your bills online? I thought so! If hacked, the culprit now has all your account information, bank information, social security number, phone number, address, all your social media accounts, driver's license number, probably even photos you've posted.

You won't even know what hit you when you're hacked. Seriously! Unless your computer begins to perform poorly, or you're suddenly missing thousands from your bank accounts, you may never know you've been hacked. On other occasions, three to four months could pass before you realize the hack took place, but by that time there's no way to track the hack.

I once felt just like you do—I thought hackers wouldn't want anything I had on my computer. I used the standard vanilla anti-virus software, and I had a firewall. I was good to go, right? Not so fast. Let me share my story.

I'm Too Small and Unimportant to be Hacked

I've had an at-home business for over 20 years. I conduct meetings in my virtual office, gather information from the companies with whom I work, send invoices for my work, and handle some confidential intellectual property of my clients. I work for clients all over the world, and up until this past year rarely gave a second thought to the possibility of my computer being hijacked. I was so naïve.

One morning while working at my computer, I was about to begin on my second cup of coffee when suddenly an annoying alert flashed on my computer. The message flashing on the screen was warning me that Microsoft had detected a significant breach in my computer and then directed me to the number in the lower right corner. I was to call their offices immediately to correct this problem, or they would have no other recourse but to shut down my computer and ban any further international activity.

Keep in mind; this was a very official looking site, complete with the Microsoft logo. I tried to shut down my computer, but when I pushed the power button, there was no response. It was completely frozen, and the warning voice was quite intimidating. So, I called the number on the screen.

The gentleman who answered the phone had a heavy east Indian accent, and his manner was quite official. He asked me if I frequently conducted international business on my computer, and I answered yes. Then he said there had been criminal activity on my computer, and they would need my cooperation to track these criminals. By this time, I was getting very suspicious, so I asked the gentleman to hang on—that I had to retrieve my password from my files. I then called my husband from my cell phone to tell him what had happened. He said, *"Get off the computer; you're being hacked!"*

I returned to the other phone, and rashly confronted the hacker. I told him I had just called my husband and he told me I was being hacked. The moment I said those words, my computer began streaming white numbers and then went to a royal blue screen. I was shocked, not knowing what to do from there. I couldn't get my computer to shut down, so I unplugged it, but by that time the damage was irreparable.

The first thing I did was run to the bank to check my accounts. Luckily, all was well there. They put an alert on my account for quite some time, just in case my bank information had been accessed. Although the banker told me that he believed it took longer for hackers to get my account information, at this point I couldn't afford to count on that piece of good news. So, I took all the precautions I knew of and returned home.

I then called a "real" representative of Microsoft to see where to go from there to retrieve the information from my computer. He told me that Microsoft would never call to tell me I was having issues with my computer. As I began to think rationally, it made perfect sense. A company that large with that many customers would never have the time to search for people with computer problems, much less call them.

After five hours of searching through my computer, I recouped very little to date, and my computer was in shambles. I lost almost all my data and business documents. My laptop still runs, if I have the time to wait an hour for it to boot. When it has sat for a long period of time and then I try to boot it, a little more information is lost with every attempt.

Fortunately, I did have all my files backed up on an external hard drive, but that too was infected because it was plugged into my computer at the time. So, I can only use this hard drive with that computer. The files that I was desperate to retrieve, I've had to retype over again to save them onto the new computer I was forced to purchase. I usually have an hour or so to copy files before the infected computer shuts down again. In fact, everything that was connected to my laptop was infected—my computer, which was just about a year old was ruined, my printer—gone, and it is still questionable how many files I'll be able to save before the infected computer gives up the ghost and dies altogether.

Microsoft told me the hackers broke through my firewall and information was streaming through the wall like water through a hole in a dike. It took only two to three minutes for the hackers to wreak this kind of havoc. Two to three minutes to destroy years of work. Amazing! I can tell you; they made a believer out of me. I will not be that naïve again.

What I have been able to recover so far is piecemeal, and the data has a good many formatting issues. What did that two-minute hack job cost me, besides my peace of mind? Well, let's examine the costs.

What Did Being Hacked Cost Me?

The hacker's damage can be assessed on several levels. For you to have a thorough understanding of what your loss could be if you were hacked, let's analyze the cost on every level.

Equipment Costs

- Computer Replacement

$1,400.00

- Hard Drive

    $ 100.00

- Printer

    $ 250.00

- Computer Diagnostics

    $ 395.00

- Data Retrieval Attempts

    $ 260.00

- Additional Future Protection for Computer

    $ 670.00

Time Loss

I averaged my costs per hour to be $50 per hour because that is my average income; however, if I would have been spending that time on marketing, my earnings had the potential to be much more. The $50 per hour is a very conservative estimate.

- Retrieval of Files (12 hrs.)

    $ 600.00

- Recreation of Files (so far 500 hrs.)

    $25,000.00

- Income Lost from Irretrievable Files (so far)

  $50,000.00
- Salary Paid for Assistant's Help (160 hrs. @$15/pr. hr.) $ 2,400.00
- Client Contact Time (250 hrs. @ $50/pr. hr.)

  $12,500.00
- Lost Income

  $85,000.00

Note: These figures are only my known costs. Who knows how much new business was lost because I was unable to serve them? I referred many people to a friend in the business. I have to believe many of the contracts she had last year was given to her during those few months I was out of commission. All I know is that my business income was down last year by $85,000.

Emotional Loss

Obviously, I was an emotional wreck for quite some time after the hackers paid me a visit. The experts told me that the hackers most likely weren't after my money or my data, all they wanted was to use my computer to stream through on their way to some other unsuspecting host. It appears that the hackers were after much bigger fish than me, I was only the vehicle used to get them to their destination. They went through my computer, and hundreds of others like mine, so that nobody could trace the future damage they were going to do back to the hackers. They used my computer to cover their tracks.

The anger, frustration, embarrassment, broken business relationships and overall personal stress I experienced was severe and relentless. I would just get over one hurdle when another would smack me in the face. Although the worst part of the anger and frustration passed soon enough, I am still suffering the embarrassment. After a year of repairing client relations, there are still customers who request information I no longer have. Then I have to drop everything I'm doing and tell them about being hacked. Not only is it embarrassing to admit, but reliving the loss is like opening up a wound over and over again. I'm emotionally raw and tender from the ongoing emotional strain caused by that brief two-three-minute encounter with a hacker.

I don't know what it was worth to the hacker, but I know what it cost me. The financial loss for last year due to the hacker was approximately $180,000, and that is a conservative estimate. The worth to the hacker had to be much more than that for him or her to take that kind of risk. Really? I guess, if the hacker was after huge corporate gains or government information, it was well worth it. The $90,000 per minute mission could have brought them millions or more. This was only figuring the cost of my computer, time, and lost information. Think of how many others were affected or "infected" who happened to be unfortunate to be in their path.

I was only one person—one small business. A study by the Small Business Association reported that 43% of small businesses are hacked in a given year, and that figure is on the rise (3).

There are literally millions of stories just like mine, or worse, that are being reported each year in the U.S. alone. Add in those who didn't report it when their computer got hacked, and the numbers grow exponentially. It's become a systemic problem, a product of our high-tech society.

According to a recent study conducted by the Center for Strategic and International Studies, up to 2014 our global economy had already paid out a whopping $575 billion at the hands of hackers (4). It's impossible for small businesses to absorb the astronomical costs of hacking, on top of their day-to-day commerce expenses. So, to whom do you think those costs are being passed? You and I—the consumer. Not only do we pay personally when our home computers are hacked, but the inflated retail prices we pay to cover the cost of corporate hacking is also a concern.

The Language of Hackers

Hackers have adopted some give-away language peculiarities that can help you to determine if you have been hacked. One of the tell-tail signs a hacker is attempting to pull the wool over your eyes is this. They typically have extremely poor grammar and spelling. Not to mention, hackers are not known for being articulate. If you suspect someone is attempting to break into your computer with a scamming hack, pay attention to the following:

- Awkward Sentence Structure
  Many hackers have been using computer language and texting far too long, which can be evident in their sentence structure. Their sentences are often fragmented—short and choppy with no clear subject or verb. Or, their sentences will run on and on, separated by comma after comma. Rarely will they use semicolons to separate complete sentences.

- Poor Organization

If you are being hacked online or an attempt to hack you is being conducted through a direct mail campaign, you will notice a rather random thought process. Their direct mail pieces or emailed promotions deliver messages that are haphazard and lack step-by-step instructions. Most of them focus more on the insignificant amount you will pay, rather than the benefits you will receive from their services.

If it's an online hacker who comes knocking, their message is usually one that is designed to motivate you to act through fear and intimidation. Hackers use bold colors and splashy messages that can initially cause you to question and doubt. The problem is, we have been taught to ignore that intuitive subconscious voice within us that recognizes the red flags. This all happens before our consciousness has the opportunity to review and analyze the information. Sometimes the best protection you have is to stop and listen to that little voice of warning.

- Poor or Inappropriate Spelling
Many promotional online appeals come from foreign hackers. People outside your country or locale will spell words differently and use unusual phraseology. For example, some spell the word "honor" like that, while others spell it "honour." Some spell "advertisement" this way, while others outside your country may spell it "advertizement." Here's a list of many words that are spelled differently, depending on the area in which you live.

Since many hackers are out of the country and unfamiliar with your colloquialisms, these words or phrases can be a dead giveaway—especially if they pretend to represent a major corporation in your country or city and use foreign spellings. Many Europeans use Johnson's Dictionary while Americans use Webster's Dictionary, which accounts for the difference in spelling. Down-right ignorance causes other differences.

European Spellings

    American Spellings

Centre

    Center

Dialogue

    Dialog

Analog Electronics

    Digital Electronics

Cancelled

    Canceled

Equalling

    Equaling

Dialled

    Dialed

Routeing

    Routing

Learnt

    Learned

Ensure

    Insure

Programme

    Program

This is assuming, of course, that the hacker knows how to spell at all. Many highly skilled hackers are only brilliant in one area— computers. Their spelling leaves a lot to be desired. If you are emailed a piece with a number of misspelled words, you have to ask yourself if this is what a reputable company would send. Would this be the type of material or direct mail pieces they would want to represent their business?

- Create Great Urgency
  When attempting to get you to act, hackers are always in a hurry, and they want you to be as well. Obviously, the quicker they can get you to respond or act, the less chance they have of being detected. Also, the more time they spend communicating with you; the

more likely they will be to make an obvious mistake that will send up a red flag. Therefore, their messages will contain words such as: *now, today, urgent, must, need, etc.*

- Create Underlying Fear or the Threat of Loss

  Hackers will tell you that you will be reported or that you will be investigated if you don't follow their instructions. Hackers will threaten to shut down your computer or even tell you that you are in danger of or have been hacked. What they fail to say is that they are the real hacker.

- Inappropriate Use of Plurals and Prepositions

  When hackers are using a foreign language, they often do not understand the rules that govern when to use plurals and prepositions. For example, let's pretend the hacker wanted to threaten you saying *"Contact Microsoft immediately, or you will be in danger of being hacked."* It might look something like this *"Contact Microsoft now, or you are in danger to be hacked."* Or, a warning like this *"People just like you have learned how to protect their computers and save their data."* It might instead read *"Peoples like you have learnt to protect there computer and save there data."* Notice the spelling errors and the inappropriate use of prepositions and pronouns (5)?

Hackers have particular days they especially love to pillage and destroy—Black Friday and Cyber Monday. These days are like Christmas for hackers. Although they take every opportunity at any given time to steal and destroy, they know you will be especially vulnerable on or around these days. Why?

A Hacker's Holiday

The reason hackers love Black Friday and Cyber Monday is that these days are technological extravaganzas. Retailers are famous for marking down the technological goodies on these two holidays, and people are out shopping, eager to purchase the latest and greatest techy toy. While shoppers are taking advantage of all the sales, hackers are taking advantage of all the shoppers—here's why?

1.   Most people who own a brand new computer haven't yet taken the time to put effective security software on it. They plug their new machines in and play for a while. It usually isn't for a few days or even weeks until they have loaded up their files that they think about how best to protect them—if at all. During this time of vulnerability, hackers have a field day. I can't tell you how many people have reported being hacked just days after purchasing a new computer.

2.   Retailers are another target for hackers during Black Friday and Cyber Monday. Think about it! All the people who are shopping and using credit cards. It's a paradise of customer information ripe for

the picking. Hackers know this, and that's why big box stores are often hacked around the holidays. Not only do they get your personal information, but they now know you have a new computer that is most likely not protected.

3. Don't feel safe if its weeks past Black Friday and Cyber Monday, and you made it through hack-free. Perhaps not! Some hackers will capture your personal credit card information, complete with name, phone number, address, and bank account balances, and they will sit on it for a while until you are feeling relatively safe and secure about not being hacked. Then, when you least expect it, they will hijack your information. You might not be any the wiser for weeks or months after the fact.

4. There are also more online purchases going on during this time. As much as retailers are advertising bargains to bring

you into the stores, hackers are advertising in a whole other way. They know that you are out there looking for bargains, so boy do they have the deal for you. Two words of caution: (a) if the offer seems too good to be true, it probably isn't true; and, (b) if the wording on the offer reads like a hacker's message, let it be a red flag to you. Most reputable companies would not allow the distribution of advertising pieces that were riddled with mistakes.

5. Hackers realize that many more people use their credit cards during the holidays than any other time of the year. For this reason, the hackers are out in numbers, lurking around your computer buys, trailing your web visits, capturing your information. They also know that retailers are busier during these times, and they are less likely to verify credit purchases than they would be during the

slow season. So, not only can they steal your card information, but their chances of getting caught are minimal.

Again, if you are careful to check your credit card purchases during the holidays, be just as diligent after the season has passed. Many hackers will wait until you're feeling safe, and then charge purchases through the roof a few weeks later when your guard is down, and your credit card statements are fuller and harder to decipher.

6.   Beware of fake Black Friday ads that direct you away from the site, asking you to take surveys. Many of these surveys are ways for hackers to gather more information. The more information hackers retrieve, the greater their chances are of successfully using your credit card and maxing out your balance. If the initial ad directs you to a site that asks for the last four numbers of your social

security card to verify credit, absolutely refuse.

I hope you understand by now that nobody is immune from hackers. After having read this book, if you are questioning whether you have been hacked—guess what? You probably have. It's that nagging little voice of reason poking at us, trying to find our better judgment that should get our attention. Intuition is not just a unique gift for women, although women are more likely to pay attention to intuition. Everybody has that prodding voice that makes them hesitate to continue in the same direction.

You have a choice to make. Do you refuse to continue when that warning voice is indicating that you may be in danger of an attack? Or, do you dismiss the fear and move forward because you don't want to be inconvenienced? Most people suspect a site or an email is not quite kosher, but they're either in a hurry or they pass it off as being paranoid. I can honestly say, I stopped for a moment and wondered whether the warning and threat on my computer screen were real. I hesitated, but then I thought nobody would want my files. They would have no meaning to another person outside the industry. That was the beginning of the end.

I'm ashamed to admit it, but there was also a certain curiosity factor that made me continue after having received the hacker's warning. I was frightened, frustrated, and curious. These are the emotional symptoms in which hackers thrive. My fears and frustrations caused me to want to end the situation quickly; however, with all the loud siren sounds and the intimidating warning voice, I was flustered and unprepared. Then I began searching for a solution. The warning on the screen offered me a way out, and I took it. I called the phone number they told me to call.

As odd as it sounds, I had this strange curiosity to know what would happen when I dialed the number. Who would answer? What would they say? Was I guilty of doing something wrong? The combination of fright, frustration, and curiosity is the thing bad "B" movies are made of—you know the kind! Where the young teenage girl hides in a dark closet upstairs, listening to the murderer as he climbs one stair at a time to loom before her just outside the closet door. All is silent! Then she does the unthinkable—she opens the door.

I could have been that teenage starlet. I instinctively knew that I was being hacked, but I just wanted the tension to go away, wanted everything to end. So, what did I do? I opened the door to the hacker.

Chapter 2: Hackers Can Be Haters

We have danced around the subject long enough, refusing to recognize that many hackers are haters. They hate government, conformists, computer illiterates, different races, sexes, rival hackers, and in many cases they hate themselves. And yet, few agencies and officials fail to call hacking crimes what they truly are—hate crimes. In fact, until hacking got so bad it was disrupting our lives and devastating corporations and governments, hacking was typically considered to be a rather harmless preoccupation of powerless people—but whom excellent at manipulating computers and individuals.

Perhaps that's what got hackers so up in arms; they didn't like the fact that others considered them to be harmless. Maybe hackers felt belittled because of their social ineptness, so they found a way to turn the tables on the rest of the world. Well, they made believers out of us all, don't you think? While many hackers are still socially awkward, lonely introverts, and closet voyeurs, there is no doubt in today's society that they are influential people seeking revenge for imagined wrongs.

Still, some people refuse to acknowledge them as criminals, thieves of our personal information, violent haters, and killers of our reputations. Instead, we smooth over and pretty up their offenses by labeling them as "hactovists" and "cyber-bullies." Would you call someone who broke into your home, robbed you, stole your identity, and destroyed your reputation and perhaps your career a bully? No, I would call them a criminal of the most cowardly kind.

The majority of hackers are haters who hide behind their computers. They look like the "all-American" boy or girl next door but don't let appearances fool you. What lurks beneath the surface is a dark current of revenge and hatred. Few have experienced this more than comedian and actress, Leslie Jones.

Not long after the release of the new "Ghostbusters," movie in which Jones starred, she was targeted by some racist trolls who viciously hacked into her social media accounts. They displayed private nude photos of her, and then placed them beside a picture of Harambe, the ape who was killed at the Cincinnati Zoo this year. Also for public viewing was Jones's phone number, address, driver's license, and a copy of her U.S. passport. Although the crimes are being investigated, it's unlikely the hackers will be caught. Like most hackers who hide their hate, they exist and travel in a subculture that few of us can navigate.

Under the Computer Fraud and Abuse Act (CFAA), if found guilty—or, if found at all—the culprits could be charged with more than 30 years. Any damages over $5,000 will earn them 10 years in prison. Another five years will be added to that sentence if the authorities can prove a conspiracy. Tack on another 15 years for stealing U.S. documents (passport) and one more for the hack being a hate crime, motivated by racial, sexual, or other prejudices.

The investigation is being handled by the U.S. Immigration and Customs Enforcement (ICE), which is the subdivision that is currently responsible for investigating computer-related activities (6) (7).

The operative words here are "if caught." Hacker haters are difficult to track because they hide in a silent, invisible world, and their personalities make them adverse to boasting about their crimes, so the majority of hackers continue to pose as your neighbors, co-workers, and loving children. They don't perceive themselves as criminals; instead, they believe they are here to right a wrong. They justify their cowardly acts by blaming others. For example, they blame Leslie Jones for taking the nude photos or being so outspoken on social media sites. Hackers believe their opinions are the only ones that should be heard; that it is their thoughts alone that have merit.

How do we locate and stop these hackers? One innovative idea is to hire other hackers to flush them out. It's like fighting fire with fire. Any given day on the Internet, you can hire rival hackers to help protect you against guys just like them. Most likely, their services are illegal, but they know how to get results. Sometimes drastic times call for drastic measures.

When I picture these hackers in this underground world, I am reminded of Hans Solo in Star Wars as he visits the bar with all the other disreputable characters just like him. Everybody is sitting at the bar or surrounding tables with their fingers on the trigger of their weapons, suspiciously eyeing anyone who enters. This is the world of hackers. Because they know and practice all the evil possibilities, they suspect everyone else of doing the same.

It's amazing to me how bold these hackers-for-hire are, advertising their illegal services and even offering competitive pricing. For a specified price, hackers will break into a generic website, social media accounts, and even create Yelp reviews designed to boost your customer base or destroy your competitor's reputation. They can post positive reviews, monitor Yelp, so the bad reviews never post, and then post poor reviews on competitor sites.

Hackers even offer to teach you how to become a novice hacker. Of course, they are only teaching the basics, nothing that would give away trade secrets within the hacking world. There was a myriad of hackers in forums and on these websites advertising their abilities to hack into Gmail accounts, Facebook, and the site even listed people who were soliciting help from the hackers, advertising the service they wanted to have fulfilled. All-in-all, it was a dark gathering of disreputes—all competing to be your criminal in waiting.

To counterbalance these hackers-for-hire, several companies are known as defenders of the web. Many have devoted their entire careers to discovering dangerous hackers, teams, and groups of hackers, designed to expose their criminal activities publicly. I'll list a few here, just in case you should ever find yourself in need.

Kaspersky Lab

Founder, Eugene Kaspersky, began his security company in 1997. Although it is headquartered in Moscow, Kaspersky boasts 30 offices all over the world. One of the most infamous hacker groups he exposed was Flame, involved in advanced cyber-espionage activities, of which Kaspersky discovered their underworld crimes in 2012. Another hacker group Kaspersky and his team uncovered was Equation Group, known for their computer spying.

FireEye

Before accepting his position with FireEye, Dave DeWalt was CEO for McAfee. FireEye is a California-based network security firm that offers threat intelligence and manages networks seeking to find any potential threats. One of FireEye's recent discoveries was a hackers group called FIN4, which was trolling Wall Street to steal insider information. His team is a dominant force in combating various malware, and he has often formed alliances with federal authorities to find the hackers' group core members.

Cylance

Stuart McClure commands this somewhat smaller company of skilled security specialists, but his skills are no less powerful. Cylance was launched in 2012, and it has some pretty impressive achievements since its infancy. One of its most noteworthy discoveries was the Iranian hacking initiative known as Operation Cleaver. They have also used their anti-malware and threat management talents using mathematics and machine learning to make a startling discovery of a widespread vulnerability in hotel Wi-Fi setups. What they found was that people who were surfing the web on hotel Wi-Fi networks were at risk of hacking. Stuart McClure has also co-authored a kind of interesting book, called "Hacking Exposed."

Trustwave

Robert McCullen heads up Trustware, which has built one of the largest information security companies. Since 1995, Trustwave's research team known as SpiderLabs has performed forensic investigations and made numerous malware discoveries. They recently uncovered a family of "point-of-sale" malware called Spark. Known for their prowess in stealing critical card data, Spark also maintained a hacker server in 2013 containing millions of stolen passwords. The company was recently acquired by another company out of Singapore for $810 million.

Palo Alto Networks

Palo Alto Networks was founded in 2005 by a gentleman named Nir Zuk. They are well known for their advanced firewalls directed toward enterprise customers. Zuk's experience as an engineer at Check Point and Net Screen Technologies have prepared him well, enabling him to discover a family of malware known as WineLunker that was targeting Apple products.

Avast

Founded in 1988 in the Czech Republic, CEO Vincent Steckler has helped to build this security company to its power since joining the team of professionals in 2009. As one of the largest security vendors, they are known around the world for their antivirus products. It was Avast who discovered significant issues with home Wi-Fi routers, and also one exploit was found in various Android Apps.

Group-IB

Founded in 2003, this Russian cyber security firm focuses on cybercrime and fraud. It's customer base stretches across more than 25 countries and is one of the largest Eastern European forensic labs in the world. The groups Head of Threat Prevention and Investigation Department is Dmitry Volkov. His involvement with Group-IB has made it indispensable to forensic investigations, claiming involvement with 80% of all high-profile investigation cases of high-tech crimes. The group's most recent activities detailed a group of hackers known as the Anunak Gang. Group-IB stopped them in their tracks, preventing further Anunak cyber crimes against the Russian banking sector.

We're in Cyber World War III, and these are the champions of our cause. They are our international generals, ready to attack the hateful hackers that are masterminding and undermining world security. They travel the same dark paths of hackers whose hate permeates every corner of the Internet. Whether we want to admit it or not, we're in the middle of a war, and our weapons are intellect, quick and thorough investigations, and people who are willing to stand against the potential damage of these revenge hackers. They risk their businesses, financial security, and lay their peace-of-mind on the line every day.

It's disheartening to think that every time you send a message, a text, or browse the web, there are hackers following closely behind waiting in the shadows to violate your right to privacy. Just because you don't see anyone hanging over your shoulder to spy on you as you text, don't think they can't see your messages. To prevent this from happening, there are apps designed especially for those whose privacy is paramount. Let's take a look at some that can give you security through almost unbreakable encryption called end-to-end.

Safest Apps to Secure Messages

- Text Secure is an Android app that was developed by Open Whisper Systems to secure texting.

- Telegram is a messaging app that is made available on Windows Phones, iOS, and Android. Two brothers in 2012 developed it. They were also responsible for launching the Russian social network VK, or VKontake. Telegram offers both normal and secure chats using end-to-end encrypting.

- Another iOS app created by Open Whisper Systems is known as Signal. Signal defends users against any external snooping to whom they might become exposed.

- Crypto Cat is also a message-sending encrypted app that is known for being user-friendly. Crypto Cat creates secure and private chat rooms using end-to-end encryption. It can be used on iOS and desktop.

- Silent Text is also a secure messaging app, developed by the same Silent Circle Company that built the Black Phone. The Black Phone's claim to fame was that it was supposed to be an NSA-snooping proof mobile device.

- Another messaging app touting complete security is Gliph. The unique feature of Gliph is that it also facilitates Bitcoin payments, allowing users to send Bitcoin currency to other Gliph users. Having this app will enable users to set message expiration times and schedule messages (8).

Don't start feeling too confident, like no hacker can penetrate all these firewalls, security software, and protective apps. Web wars have a way of changing the course of technology. One day you feel well-armored—the next day your privacy is hacked to the bone. Cyber wars have left a trail of victims whose lives were forever altered by the hackers' hateful activities. There is no question that hackers have incredible talent, are highly intelligent, but for some reason, they have chosen to use these gifts to attack the innocent. The little guys, like you and I, are victim to their sieges, their computer carnage, and their message marauding.

More puzzling than the Darth Vaders of the hackers' world are those of us who continually refuse to employ even the simplest of security systems. It is nonsensical to imagine that a password using your pets name and your birthdate is going to protect you, and yet we do it all the time. If that isn't bad enough, we use the same password for all our accounts, making it that much easier for a hacker to break into one and all. We know, and yet we choose to ignore the advice of the experts on how to protect our data and accounts, how to hold on to our privacy.

Perhaps it's that we don't believe a few little things are going to make any difference.

Hackers are going to hack. So, we turn the other way and keep our fingers crossed that the hacker won't select our computer, our phone, or our social media accounts to do their evil deeds. What's even more amazing is the surprise and shock we experience when we do get hacked. Really? Like the rules were made for everyone else but us. We're like ostriches who have buried our heads in the sand. The problem is we've all lost our minds to the sand worms.

Like a dark ally in a dangerous neighborhood, there are places on the Internet that we should not visit. There are bad neighborhoods, riddled with wild beasts waiting to devour your data. Even practicing some common sense strategies can give you some protection.

Common Sense Strategies to Protect You on the Web

The majority of people who are hacked fail to practice the following simple strategies that could have given them a small measure of protection. Even a little protection is better than none. So, if some of the things we have covered seem too complicated or cumbersome, here are some easy ways to practice cyber safety.

1. Be mindful of what you download or install on your computer. Hackers can be quite clever. They routinely disguise themselves to resemble security guards for hire, pretending to defend you against users like them.

2. Treat emails from unknown sources with caution, especially ones that sound like they're a greeting from an old friend. Subject lines that read *"Hey, I finally found you,"* or *"Can't wait to see you again,"* are hackers' favorite ploys. Make a promise to yourself—if you don't recognize the source of the email, don't open it.

3. Use at least two different browsers. One can be used for surfing, playing games,

watching YouTube, or anything that doesn't require a login. Use your other browser for all your important things that require a login. Keeping them separate will help to prevent web tracking.

4. Since online hackers often infect computers when you view advertisements, use Adblock or Adblock Plus when you surf the web.

5. Keep your computer updated. Windows and Mac regularly offer free upgrades; take advantage of them. Machines that are using old browsers or outdated systems are open-door invitations to hackers.

6. Backup everything, and don't forget to detach the backup device when it is not in use. When computers are infected, it can pass through to all the attached devices, including your printer. A crashing computer can take any external hard drives with it, so unplug.

7.   Keep a copy of your photos on a CD. That way, should something happen to your computer, you won't have lost all your irreplaceable pictures as well.

8.   We've already discussed using hard to guess passwords, and you've been warned not to use the same password for all your accounts. It may be a little more inconvenient to write them all down and keep them in a safe place, but one day you may be glad you did (9).

Are All Hackers Bad?

Not all hackers are evil; not all web surfers are good. It all depends on your perspective. If you're looking to hire a hacker, his or her ethics are probably your last concern. Asking if there are any good hackers are like asking if there are friendly cancer cells. All hackers spread into unwanted areas where they don't belong. All hackers start doing one little thing, and before you know it they have infected your entire body of technology. Every hacker, at one time or another, would like to be free of his or her technological disease, but their cyber-sickness has taken over their sense of fair play.

So, I'll just show you the three known types of hackers and let you be the judge.

White Hat Hackers

These are the necessary good-guy hackers who make war with the bad hackers. They usually work in security firms or are students whose goal is to make the world a safer place. They often discover criminal hackers and report them to the authorities. Then they develop a fix for the breach and sell it to people who have been hacked. Are they all good? Well, probably not all good—but necessary.

White Hat hackers are easy to hire, contracted to protect and defend your privacy. Computer security firms employ them. Since they are hacking experts, they won't be cheap. Be prepared to pay handsomely for the services you request. My complaint with some White Hat hackers is that they can be a bit arrogant and feel quite self-important, knowing the general public has no idea of how they do what they do.

Black Hat Hackers

The only Black Hat hackers you can locate are most usually those who want to be found. Those for hire can be accessed on Reddit, and because of their over-inflated egos they like to brag about their hacking prowess. Social forums, Twitter, and chat groups harbor hackers; you can try phishing for your hacker in one of these locations.

Grey Hat Hackers

These type of hackers act like double agents—sometimes White Hat hackers, and sometimes Black Hat hackers. Some believe Grey Hat hackers are the most untrustworthy of all. You never really know who's showing up. Is it the hacker that is going to help you, or is it the hacker who is going to screw you over? Like the White Hat hackers, Grey Hat hackers are usually easy to locate. Remember to watch your back, though, if you should decide to use their services. Apply the "one eye open" kind of trust when it comes to dealing with Grey Hat hackers (10).

A word to the wise, avoid accepting files or downloads from any hacker you have contacted for help. Even those who have offered to teach you. A hacker cannot resist hacking; they're addicted to snooping, and you could be their next target. Even if they call themselves friends, resist. Even if you've known them for years, keep them at arm's length. Trusting a hacker is like sleeping with a python. They are attracted to your warmth, and they curl around you for slumbering comfort but beware. They could be sizing you up for their next meal.

It may also be a good thing to question why it is that you wish to hire a hacker. If hackers are haters, involved in all sorts of diabolical activities, why is it you want or need to go to the dark side? Before contacting a hacker, search every other avenue to get the information you need another way. Whether you need to retrieve a password, access a social media account, or hack into an email account, why is it you feel you have the right to invade another's privacy? Even if you believe your intentions to be honorable, I'm sure you've heard that there is no honor among thieves. Isn't that what you're doing? Stealing another's information doesn't make you any better than the hacker.

It's been my experience that doing something right, but going about it the wrong way, has a way of coming back to bite you on the backsides. Most of the time, hacking into someone else's life is the coward's way. Wouldn't it be better to take the high road, to obtain information honestly and with integrity? Think about it! If you are so willing to compromise your principles for this one thing, what's to come tomorrow? What lengths will you be prepared to go the next time you are in need?

Should you choose to hack, you will find people who will commiserate with you. However, you might see a side of them and yourself that you never knew existed. It's a dark and sinister side, a lonely path that once traveled is difficult to find your way home again. Once you give into the thrill or convenience of hacking, it can slide and slither its way into your life in many other forms. The life of a hacker is not experienced first-hand but rather taken one little piece at a time from the fuller lives of others. So, before entering that world, ask yourself if hacking is your only option. Will you respect yourself in the morning?

Chapter 3: Hidden in Plain Sight

Have you ever seen camouflage paintings or drawings? Interestingly enough, they first appear to be one thing, but upon closer inspection, the scene is something completely different? There is an artist named Jonathan Talbot who does such sketches. Years ago I became fascinated with his work. One of my favorites was his depiction of a New York City skyline. From a distance, it looked like the city's skyline done in shades of white, gray, and black. Most intriguing was that the closer you got, the less it looked like a cityscape. Instead, the picture changed right before my eyes. Suddenly, the skyline was transformed into famous people and landmarks. Each scene depicted memorable New York City events, shop fronts, and restaurants, and neighborhoods. From Little Italy to Times Square, each small scene blended to produce one shadowy skyline. The Empire State Building was recognizable from afar, but up close it became people, signs, hanging fish, markets—a myriad of separate pictures. It was a hundred scenes contained with the one picture. Fascinating!

My preoccupation with camouflage art has continued throughout the years. Just recently I was enamored with a television program that featured body art. Artists would take their subjects into grocery stores, libraries, and wine shops. There they would pose their subjects before displayed products and paint their bodies to blend in with the food, bottles, or shelved books. It was unbelievable. Looking at their finished work, the painted person became part of the display. It was challenging to see where one left off and the other began.

These visions are what I imagine when discussing the possibilities of hackers being able to hide beneath and between the layers of your computer and go undetected. Not only is it done with malware, but also with software and techniques, we will talk about later on in this chapter. The hackers performing this magic are not necessarily changing the code; they are simply hiding in plain sight. Like an arsonist leaving the fire he set with nobody being the wiser. He simply dresses like a firefighter and walks out the front door in the midst of all the chaos. Much like the hacker who travels along your computer's pathways, hidden in plain sight.

Even experts hired to snoop inside your computer to discover the hackers trap don't see the problem because it's unexpectedly in plain sight. However, it blends into the background code or hides in the most obvious place thereby being overlooked. Because most people or businesses don't have a baseline of what is normal to use as a comparison, the hacker can slide in without making any noticeable changes that would send out a security alarm. We mistakenly believe that what we cannot see, doesn't exist.

Hackers have perfected the art of hiding messages right out in the open. It's called steganography, and hackers have used this tool to turn mayhem up to a whole new level. Steganography is a form of cloaking code hidden within something else. It's nothing new; spies have used steganography for over a thousand years. Steganography is when you hide something right out in the open. Think of it as a type of camouflage, only much more clever.

Steganography comes from the Greek, and it means concealed writing. It was used in Roman times to hide messages and even Bible passages in ancient wax tablets. Unlike scrambled cryptography information that cannot be understood, steganography blends right in, camouflaging the information, so the user doesn't even know it's there. Hackers cover their messages up with written text, images, video, encoded messages, almost anything to divert the user's attention. It's quite an art, but one that can be your undoing. They are virtually impossible to detect. There is no trace of them, nothing that would indicate to the user that a hacker's message was resting and waiting to be awakened when needed. There is nothing on the surface, no encrypted messages or coded clues that would lead one to believe that havoc is lurking beneath a clean surface.

Absolutely thousands of steganography tools are available to hackers, and many hackers will go to any lengths to keep their secrets hidden. It is their objective to remain hidden. Steganography offers them a way to keep their secrets safe by carefully covering their tracks. The better and more successful the cybersecurity gets, the more techniques the hacker will adopt to avoid detection. It's like a game of cat and mouse; however, security companies want to be the cat; it's the mouse who eventually gets caught and devoured (11).

Obviously, hackers can be and are hidden right under our noses and we never even know they are there. It's not like they send us a greeting to let us know they're paying us a visit. It's a sobering thought, but there's a good chance that many of you, right now, are being watched as you read this book. The eyes of underworld hackers are everywhere, even right in plain sight. We just don't know what to look for, and so the hackers sleep in our computers until awakened to wreak havoc on our systems when we least expect it and are ill-prepared to handle their onslaught.

Whether you are a government agency, a retail store, a gamer, or a busy bee who uses the computer as a work tool, no one is exempt from the clever hacker. They are no respecter of persons. A stay-at-home mom is just as susceptible to a hack attack as the CEO of a major corporation. We're are all at the mercy of hackers, and the best we can do to subvert their hold over our computers is to educate ourselves. Knowing how hackers fly under the radar will offer us at least a moderate amount of protection.

Evasive Techniques of the Hacker

It's important to know that not all hackers use invasive malware (software designed to damage your computer) as they maneuver through the darkened alleys of your machine. They are much cleverer than that. Many are not out to destroy as yet; they would rather stay around for a while to spy on your activities and reap the benefits of lurking around in the shadows until the time is right. Then they pounce, stealing your secrets, discoveries, and private information. Like night stalkers, they may want to know your secret haunts, to use them against you at a more opportune time. Therefore, instead of leaving a path of destruction, they cleverly open avenues of passage where they can freely enter and leave your computer at will without you ever having been the wiser.

Let's take a look at how some hackers enter and leave your system at will, shopping through your files for any information that could be used later down the road to damage your reputation or extort money.

Did You Open the Door to A Hacker?

Nobody opens the door to a hacker and invites them in for a cup of data and a piece of information pie. However, hackers have their ways of accessing your computer. They certainly don't wait for an invitation. All they need is an unlocked door, a cracked window, or an inconspicuous entrance to squeeze into your computer. Some of the most popular and more common methods hackers are using to access your computer are as follows.

Phishing

One of the most fruitful and efficient ways of hacking into your computer is through email phishing. Here's how it works. The hacker will send official looking emails in mass, appearing to be from a bank or some online payment site. Recipients are instructed to verify their account information by clicking on the particular link.

Once the person who received the email clicks on that link and provides their login information, it's all over. You've just opened the door and invited the hacker to come in and steal all your account information.

For some of you more savvy computer users, you're probably wondering what fools would fall for that one, right? The answer to that question is about 0.4 percent of the people targeted do as they are told and provide the information. Oh, that's not that many, you say. Oh no? Think again. If 100,000 people were emailed, the statistics say that 400 unsuspecting people will fall for the hacker's ploy.

If you are an individual, reading this book because you want to know how to protect and defend your privacy, don't stop there. Tell your family members and friends what you learn. Remember, there's power in numbers. The more knowledge you share with others, the more informed everyone will become. If you are a business owner, you cannot afford to leave your people in the dark. If I were you, I'd make sure they all received a copy of this book and make it required reading. After all, it just takes one employee to compromise your entire computer networking system.

Remind family members and co-workers always to be on the watch for suspicious looking email attachments. Warn them about the dangers of pop-up screens that ask for personal or company information. Educate your friends, family members, and business associates that hackers often pose as authoritative figures who can only help them if they share personal or confidential information.

The Password Hack

Okay, so this is the third time we have talked about the importance of creating passwords that are random, that don't include personal information, that should frequently be changed, that should not be the same on every account, and that use a combination of letters, numbers, and special characters. Implementing these strategies will at least give the hacker a bit of a challenge. Although there is no failsafe way to prevent a skilled hacker from obtaining your password, a little bit of discouragement will go a long way. We hope by the third mention of the importance of password protection, you'll begin to understand the importance of practicing these methods.

Warning! Downloading Free Software Isn't Always Free

There is a familiar adage that you get what you pay for. By attempting to download free software, you'll most likely get a whole lot more than you bargained for secretly tucked inside the software. The hacker will be happy to share dangerous malware, viruses, or "bugged" software that will make you wish you would have paid the upfront costs.

In many cases, those who design and offer this free software don't just provide this because they want to help you out. They want to help themselves to your computer. It's always a good idea to ask yourself—*"Why would a person or company I don't know, want to give me something for nothing? What's in it for them?"* If you see no advantage to the one offering the freebie, be careful. There may be something in it for you that you hadn't counted on receiving (12).

Practicing Probe a Dope

Sounds a little harsh, I know, but hackers are always trolling for weaknesses in your computer. Those who have compromised firewalls, old software and unprotected computers scream "I'm yours" to the hacker. Hackers are gamblers; they play the numbers game. If they send emails to enough systems, They'll find some that are malfunctioning, misconfigured, or un-patched. So, did you invite the intruding hacker—yep!

Refuse to fall victim to the "probe a dope" game that hackers play by keeping your software and machine updated and its defenses strong.

Hackers Are Social

Well, perhaps not social in the way you and I expect, but they love to snoop on social media sites. It's common practice for hackers to create an impressive sounding fake profile that is designed to entice even the most resolved loner. From there, they lead you down the dark alley that links to malicious websites. Before you know it, you've been duped into divulging your personal information.

Hacker Hijacking Ads

Resist clicking on a lot of ads; you never know which ones contain code designed to hijack your computer. Cyber criminals often place these ads on legitimate websites and wait for an eager participant. Some show photos that peak your curiosity, and some advertise wonder creams or procedures that are hard to resist. Two words of advice, when you find yourself hanging your finger over the ad, and you feel as though you can't resist—try harder! Remember what curiosity did to the cat (13)!

Now the Real Fun Begins!

Once the hacker is "in," the real fun begins. Well, maybe fun for them—for you, life as you know it is about to go sideways for a while. What can be accomplished in just a brief little visit will knock your socks off. Hackers can use your computer in ways you've never even considered. Once in, the hacker can . . .

- Use your computer with others they have gathered to form a larger network of hijacked machines and use them to attack banks, entities, military targets, and governments.

- Snoop traffic channels on your computer to identify credit card processing servers.

- Abduct all the contacts in your email folders to create mayhem by spreading viruses, spyware, and malware to friends, family members, and co-workers.

- Involve your computer and you in illegal or illicit activities without your knowledge.

- The hacker can hijack every username and password typed on your keyboard. They can capture the logins for bank accounts and then carry out online transactions to steal your money (14).

You can't discuss hackers without introducing those little monsters they use to infiltrate your computers—malware. We've mentioned malware, but just in case you have never been exposed to it and aren't sure what is meant by malware, it never hurts to have a bit more information on the subject. Malware is a combination of two words that will give you a good idea of how bad it is—it's short for malicious software. Hackers use this software to disrupt the operation of your computer or computer systems. The malware allows hackers to gain access to sensitive, private information or display unwanted information about you to the public (15).

Malware is the general term that refers to a host of nasty software intended to cause you a boatload of issues. Before coining the term malware, we used to lump it all together and call all the different types of malware a "computer virus." Now we know that calling all forms of malware a virus is like grouping diseases such as cancer, diabetes, kidney failure, and the common cold all together and calling them that "sickness." It's important to know the different types of malware to help you identify their sources and gain at lease a teaspoon of prevention against their probable attacks.

The following are some of the most popular and too often experienced forms of malware.

Viruses and Worms

These types of malware are specifically named for the infectious manner in which they are spread. A computer virus nests in another executable software, which is most often your operating system. As soon as you run your machine, the virus spreads to selected programs. A worm works a bit differently, although just as disastrous. It is a stand-alone malware program that spreads its infection from your computer to the other machines in your network. The virus spreads by an unaware user running the infected program or operating system. The worm is a more independent creature; it spreads itself (16).

Trojan Horses

Like the Trojan Horse in ancient times, this type of malware program appears interesting or useful to entice its victims to install. Once installed, Trojan Horses viciously invade your computer. They are hidden to the user, so the only side effect you may notice is a slower performing computer. Unlike viruses or worms, Trojan Horses don't spread into other files (17).

Rootkits

Rootkits act like a magic cloak to conceal malicious programs after they are successfully installed. Some Rootkits hide while others contain routines that prevent removal (18).

Backdoors

Backdoors are invisible to the user, another tool that is hidden in plain sight. Backdoors provide hackers with ways to bypass authentication procedures, usually over an Internet connection. Once compromised, the hacker will use one or more backdoors that offer them future access to your machine or network. Backdoors are often installed by implants, Trojan horses, and worms (19).

Evasion

One of the most popular ways for today's hackers to fly under the radar is through Stegomalware. Stegomalware is a sophisticated way to enable hackers to secretly place malware components with specific resources. Whenever they wish to use the malware, the hacker can use evasion to bring them out undetected to spy, destroy, or gain future access to information (20).

Along with frequently backing up your computer and using virus and spyware protective programs, there is also specifically designed software and a variety of measures you can take to help protect you against hackers' malware attacks. Perhaps just knowing these exist will give you hope in what can seem like a hopeless situation.

Anti-virus and Anti-malware Software

Anti-virus and anti-malware software digs deep down into your computer and hides in the same dark neighborhoods where malware lives. Every time the user opens a file, the anti-virus or anti-malware software scans it for legitimacy. If the file doesn't check out, the user will be notified. These anti-malware programs defend your computer in two significant ways: (a) provides real-time protection against the installation of malware; or, (b) detects and removes malware that has already been unknowingly installed (21).

Website Security Scans

These alerts have been provided by website developers to prevent malware infections passed through their site onto browsers' machines. Companies have no wish to damage their reputations or be blacklisted by search engines for hosting malware. For this reason, they have employed scans that check their websites for malware and report potential security issues to browsers.

"Air Gap" Isolation or "Parallel Network"

To put it lightly, these are methods to isolate the user from the network. What do you do? Disconnect your machines from the network and create a "gap" between you and your neighboring machines. Oh but wait, you don't think hackers would be put off so easily, do you? They have figured out ways to mind the gap. We now know that information from air-gapped computers can be leaked, but the methods are somewhat challenging, even for the most determined hackers.

Then There's a Gray Area

The gray area is known as Grayware. Grayware is not as notorious as malware, but it can hinder your computer's performance and cause unnecessary security risks. Among others included in Grayware are items like spyware, joke programs, adware, and remote access tools. While not as severe as malware, Grayware can create annoying and inconvenient computer performance.

The first thing to do when you discover malware hiding within your computer is to have yourself a 5-minute panic attack. Okay, now take a deep breath and realize that this doesn't have to mean the loss of every personal file or the public display of all your personal information. Your life is not over; all may not be lost! Before you sentence your machine to death by burying it in a closet for the rest of its days, try these ten things that might restore its healthy functioning.

Ten Things to Do After Discovering Malware On Your Computer

1. Backup all your personal files. You may have
        already done so, and that's a good thing.
        A word of warning, be sure you're not
        backing up infected files.

2.   Disconnect from the Internet. Unplug the
Ethernet cable or disable your Wi-Fi.

3. Boot in Safe Mode or use an Antivirus Rescue
Disk. Here's how you get to Safe Mode:

- Restart Computer.
- Press and hold the F8 Key as your
  computer boots.
- If Safe Mode isn't already selected, use
  your arrow key to navigate to it.
- Press Enter.
- Once you're in Safe Mode, continue
  malware removal. If Windows won't
  start, then you'll need to use an
  antivirus rescue disk.

4.   Get another computer with Internet
access.

- Put computers side-by-side so that you can search the Internet on your clean computer. You'll need to do this to research problems and symptoms of the infection once it has been identified. You may also need to download specific programs to remove the infection.
- Use a blank flash drive to transport downloaded programs to the infected computer.

5. Try to identify the malware and search for files.

- If possible, discover the name of the malware.
- Once you've found its name, research until you find removal instructions.
- You can also employ "MakeUseOfAnswers" to assist you.

6. Make sure no more infections are found by scanning with a variety of programs.

- Don't worry if you cannot find anything about the suspected infection.
- There are several removal tools you can use, from antivirus to Rootkit. You can also use anti-adware and anti-spyware, or implement general anti-malware programs to clear your computer.

7. Do A Clean-up On Your Computer

- Some of the recommended software includes CCleaner, Xleaner, and Drive Tidy.
- Then, comb through your programs list with an app like GeekUnInstaller to get rid of any potentially dangerous software.

8. Remove System Restore Points

- Although this can be a useful tool, you don't want to take the chance that it will contain malware--so delete it.

9.   Fix Post-malware Removal Problems

- You ought to try Microsoft's Fix It Tool to fix the problems.
- You could also try Re-Enable II to do the job.

Note: If these issues still occur, you can try MakeUseOfAnswers again for additional help.

a.   Computer is still slow

b.   Homepage is different

c.   Cannot connect to the Internet

d.   Windows Update and Firewall won't work

e.   Search Engine is redirecting you to random Websites

f.   Missing Desktop Icons

g.   Programs and/or files won't open

10.   Change Your Passwords

Getting rid of malware can be frustrating and time-consuming, so be patient. Of course, it's always better to use preventative measures than to try to patch and mend after the fact. Being aware of nasty malware trolls that are hidden in plain sight gives you the knowledge needed to help you stop hackers in their tracks.

Chapter 4: The Chaotic Aftermath

It's amazing how a two-minutes attack can have a two-month or more aftermath of chaos and loss. Depending on whether the assault is toward an individual, an organization, business, or a government agency, the hackers can destroy and even shut down an entire group. If you have a good deal of personal funds to replace equipment and restore the damage, you might survive the attack. However, if you're a small business running on a shoestring budget, it could cause you to close your doors

 permanently.

To see how well prepared you are to weather the storms of a hacker, let's examine the effects on different entities and individuals and what to do with all the confusion afterward. Almost as important as what your losses could and probably will be if you are hacked, is the fact that you will need to take protective measures to assure it won't happen again. Many people who have reported being hacked find themselves in the precarious position of being victimized again shortly after the first attack.

Like burglars who rob a home and steal electronics and valuable personal items, the hackers have learned how easy it is to attack the same people or companies again. The hackers are patient, though. They always give you time to replace destroyed servers and gather more data before a repeat performance. If you are an individual who was hacked, the culprit will give you time to replace or repair your machine and then plant more malware. Why the repeated attacks? The easiest explanation is that they can.

After restoring their data and repairing their computers, many individuals and organizations are misled into believing that they're safe. They sigh a deep breath of relief, fix a few things, and then it's business as usual. In many cases, the measures taken to ensure the hackers don't return are minimal. The protection received from the implementation of these policies aren't much better. Sadly, most of us just aren't educated regarding preventative and post-hack detection and security methods.

Since hackers' work and purposes are significantly different between private home office or personal data attacks and that of businesses or governmental agencies, we'll examine each one separately.

When Hackers Attack the Individual

Hackers most favorite targets are home and home office computers. If these computers are connected to the Internet by broadband, even better. Broadband connections give hackers greater opportunities to locate these type of computers with scanners, and the access channel is always open to them. Although we've already discussed the ways hackers attack, and we've shown you what they could do to your systems, data, and finances, our aftermath instructions are not yet complete.

Common sense will tell you that you need to verify that your banking information is intact and that you are not passing on the dangerous malware through your computer to your contacts, but how do you handle the aftermath. You may not have a business to lose, but the emotional toll from hacking can be tremendous. Hackers know how to prey on people's emotions to encourage participation without most of us being any the wiser.

One of the most valued players in an organized hacking group is what is known as their social engineer. Social engineering campaigns are designed to tap into the recipient's emotions to create an opening for them to access your information. There are typically five different emotions hackers use to gain compliance. They are as follows.

1.   Fear

2.   Obedience

3.   Helpfulness

4.   Greed

5.   Need to Belong

The success rate is phenomenal for hackers who can socially engineer or manipulate one's emotions to gain access to information. It's a psychological game, which is played upon the weaknesses and personal needs of those who fall victim to their attacks. Hackers have discovered that by tapping into these five human emotions and needs, they can exploit and manipulate users into providing a myriad of information. Let's examine these feelings closer, shall we?

Achieving Compliance Through Fear

It can be quite intimidating for anyone to believe there are hackers out there whose primary goal is to sabotage them and their technology. Nobody wants to believe some people just want to create emotional pain and financial suffering. Hackers have an incredible grasp on how to manipulate individuals by creating fearful situations. They'll even send you an email or text in the pretense that they are protecting you against an eminent hacker attack. All along, they are the offenders.

The primary sources of fear that hackers use on individuals are as follows.

Fear of Loss

This could be the fear of lost property, privacy, reputation, or financial well-being. Hackers know how to play upon these fears to motivate you to comply with their demands. Once they have threatened you with exposure or loss, they blackmail you into doing their bidding.

Fear of the Unknown

Our imaginations can be a beautiful thing, but when the emotions run wild, we can be paralyzed by pictured disasters and the unknown results of being hacked. If you're going to let fear of the unknown motivate you to act, do so as a preventative measure, not as a knee jerk reaction to a hacker's threats. Refuse to allow yourself to be held ransom because you are afraid of something that you don't even know will happen. The fear itself is often worse than the unknown issues you are imagining.

Fear of Disappointment

Some of us are so afraid we'll miss out on an offering and be disappointed, we act without considering the consequences. Social engineers who prey on this type of fear usually do so by coding an ad that promises you something amazing. Fearing disappointment if you don't take advantage of the offering, the individual clicks on the ad for further investigation. Bingo—the hacker has now gained access to your machine.

Fear of Ridicule

Hackers who are expert at social engineering know what to say and do to make you feel like less of a person if you don't follow their instructions. For example, they may send you an email that says something like this: *"You'll never guess what your friends are saying about you."* Afraid that your friends are making fun of something you did or said, you are tempted to click on the email. Don't do it—not even if you're just curious to discover what the email's all about—avoid feeding the fear or even the curiosity.

Fear of Rejection

Hackers know almost every computer has information its user wouldn't want to be made public. So, they threaten exposure to this information unless you comply. Hackers may not have the power they are pretending to have; they can achieve these things if you let them tap your fears and then give them access to the very information you fear they'll obtain. The best idea is not to keep such private information on your computer—within a finger's reach of the hacker.

Access Through Obedience

Knowing that most people feel compelled to obey an authoritative figure, hackers will often create a situation where they pose as an official or organization who could cause you great harm if you refuse to submit to their demands. Just recently, some of these hackers have used the IRS to threaten and scam people out of vast sums of money. They warn them that if they fail to pay a specific amount of money, chances are the IRS will conduct an audit. Or, they place a warning on your screen telling you that you have been the victim of a cyber attack, and then instruct you to call the specified number to avoid complete computer failure. What do we do—we obey, and the hackers get access to our computers.

Access Because of Our Greed

Almost all of us would like to have a little more of things—more money, more recognition, or more time. When the want is balanced with the knowledge that those things typically come from hard work and dedication, we are much less likely to be targeted by the "get it quick" schemes of hackers. Hackers who manipulate through greed will usually promise wealth or rare possessions if you follow some simple instructions. Some hackers have promised lottery wins, trips, car giveaways, and even posed as Publisher's Clearing House representatives to get money. They request a small amount of money paid to them for shipping or the release of items. Of course, the items are never to follow. Again, if the offering seems too good to be true—resist the temptation. Don't let greed overrule your better judgment.

Access by Requesting Help

Hackers are notorious for asking for help, and most of us have a need to help others. Be careful though when the request requires you to divulge or accept information that could cause your privacy to be compromised. This happened to one of Amazon's customer support representatives. The hacker appealed to the customer support person, asking for help. He already had his victim's name and email address. All he needed now was an account. So, he chatted up the employee, and before long he had achieved his goal. The hacker soon gained access to the shopper's credit card information and made some expensive purchases on Amazon. It was devastating to the customer as well as the employee who fell for the hacker's request for help (22).

Access Because Of Your Need to Belong

One of our greatest human needs is to belong. We want to belong to a family, an organization, a cause, etc. Hackers prey on this need, inviting us to join this cause or that group, and all you have to do is fill out the application or survey. On the survey, however, you're divulging private and valuable information that the hacker will use to access your data and personal information. Avoid joining online promotional memberships unless you are familiar with the organization and you know they are reputable.

For individual users, the emotional toll after an attack can be just as devastating as the financial and data loss. Make a vow to yourself that your emotions will not rule you should you become a victim of a hacker's attempts take advantage of you when you're in an emotional state. Be a savvy user, and recognize the effort before it turns into a full-blown attack.

When Hackers Attack Small Businesses

Unlike many larger corporations, today's small businesses may find it difficult to protect themselves or prevent hackers from wreaking havoc. What is worse, the hack will often destroy their ability to repair the damage and calm the chaos, eventually causing them to shut down their operations. Let's see how small businesses can defend themselves against the ever-increasing threat of hackers.

Preventative Measures

We've talked about the importance of security, but many small business owners believe they cannot afford to protect their data. The cost of security experts can be too much for them to absorb into their budget. For entrepreneurs who feel defeated before they open their doors because they need but cannot afford the protection, don't give up on your dreams because of the hacker. There are other methods of protecting data that are reasonable and easy to achieve.

One such method is to educate yourself and your employees. Set up company policy about what to do if you suspect an attack. This will empower your staff, giving them confidence in knowing what to look for and what to do about a suspected hack. In fact, give them a copy of this book and then go through some hacking scenarios. Practice what to do in case of an attempt to access information. Educate them on what information that it's never a good idea to provide. All employees should know your expectations. If they are in question of an email or communication requesting sensitive information, then they should defer to upper management.

During the Hack

When there is a successful hack, let your employees know what your policy will be. What should they do to prevent widespread damage? What symptoms will they experience that indicate a potential or possible hacking? Now is not the time to blame employees, even when they have a direct responsibility in unintentionally allowing the hacker to access data or intellectual information.

If employees don't feel safe to communicate their suspicions, the hacker's job will be made so much easier. Who do you think is going to report a problem in booting their computer or an inefficient machine if they fear reprisal from upper management? The best thing you can do is make your employees feel comfortable in reporting an issue that could be evidence of a hacker's attack.

The Aftermath

If your business cannot afford an IT department or team, you may need to have consultants come in after the hackers have done their dirty deed to clean up and restore. The cost of IT may be less than doing nothing and opening your business up to another hack. If you are located near a university, you might want to talk to their computer science college and see if you can hire an intern or a student near graduation that could help you out. It would provide some excellent experience for the student and offer an inexpensive way for you to satisfy your security needs as well.

Expect some pretty massive aftermath in your business, not only with your systems and doing damage control with customers—but, your employees may feel insecure as well. Not only do you have personal information on your computer about clients; but, most likely, all your employee information has also been compromised. If there are some that feel responsible for causing the breach, they may take the brunt of the criticism from co-workers and management. Be prepared for some fallout in your workers, if you haven't communicated your expectations in case of a hack.

The most effective and efficient way to handle hackers is to stress to everyone the importance of backing up your data each day. Also, don't give every employee full access to sensitive information. Warn workers to be thoughtful about what they post online, whether at work or home. Explain to them the importance of frequently updating their systems. You may also consider hiring that student intern to provide some basic prevention hands-on instruction for your workers to teach them how to protect themselves against a probable hack.

Just because you have avoided any cyber attacks so far, this is no time to become apathetic. Stay alert and informed. Be familiar with some of the latest reported hackers and scams to keep all your people educated (23). Some of the things you, as the boss, will need to be cognizant of after an attack is that there will be a lot of activity going on at the same time as you're trying to conduct regular business. Here are some of the things you might have to deal with during the aftermath of hacking.

- Time lost investigating and repairing damage
- Standard business transactions will take more time
- You will have trust issues with customers and employees

- Depending on the seriousness of the breach, you may have some legal issues to handle.
- You will have additional expenses in IT or security help.

The Aftermath of Governmental Agency Hacks

It's an ominous thought to realize that bold and talented hackers could threaten the safety of an entire nation. Political hacking has risen to a whole new level of late. The U.S. can give testimony to the dangers of political hacking, with those being committed last week against the Democratic National Committee. Here we are, only weeks before the presidential election, and agencies are reporting breaches of the Democratic National Committee and the Democratic Congressional Campaign Committee.

This is no small feat, but rather one that would need the backing of high-ranking officials to break through the advanced security these agencies employ. Top Democrats on the House and Senate Intelligence panels are convinced that Russian officials are attempting to influence or sway U.S. elections with these hired hackers. They have now stolen and posted emails on Wikileaks, DCLeaks.com and Guccifer 2.0. The power of these hackers is disconcerting, thinking that it might be possible for them to manipulate, delete, or in some way influence the outcome of our votes (24).

It is unconscionable to think that the aftermath of these types of hacks could determine the future of a nation. The problem is, we have become way too comfortable with the trust we place in our computers. We dump every detail of classified information into our government systems and then foolishly feel betrayed when the computer relays that information to others. Newsflash, computers have no loyalties. They have no conscience, no feelings of remorse or guilt should information they contain get in the hands of dangerous criminals or radical leaders.

If we are to continue to place such trust in our computers, to consider them to be discreet and loyal subjects, then we deserve what we get—hacked. When it comes to the world-wide-web, we need a reality check. We must understand that everything that is put on a website or stored in a file can and will in all probability will be hacked. When it comes to the hackers, nothing is truly classified—nothing is top secret, and understanding this truth is the first step to your ability to defend yourself against hackers.

One would think all this knowledge of government's intelligence agencies hacking into one another's systems, that the security measures taken would send the snooper packing. Not so! Hack attacks are on the rise at an incredible rate. A survey of 24 federal agencies confirmed that from 2006 to 2015, cyberattacks exploded to over a 1,300%. Attacks are getting more sophisticated, efficient, and numerous as well, with hackings climbing to $77,000 during 2015 (25). It's turned into hackers' heaven, and we're all in danger of falling into the pit.

If you're not a business owner, and a corporate hacker has not exposed your personal information, you may mistakenly believe that these security breaches will not affect your day-to-day life. If you want to continue in that belief, then perhaps there is little we can do to change your mind. However, now that the government is involved in hacks, you must admit to the potential adverse effects this could directly have on you and your family.

If it is true that hackers could rig a national election, just think of the repercussions of such a find. If people believed the votes were rigged, eventually who would even bother to vote?

Okay, so we keep talking about educating yourself and your employees, but how? We have listed some resources below that will assist you in gaining knowledge and keeping you current with the latest scams, hacks, and methods used in today's wacky world of hackers.

Resources to Keep You Current with the Hackers' Latest Schemes

Since hackers and their offensive schemes are always shifting and evolving, you can use these resources to stay abreast of many of the current methods they could implement to access your information.

Security Bloggers Network

Security Bloggers Network is just what it says—a network of security bloggers that discuss a broad range of security topics that you need to hear.

Darknet

Darknet is a blog that turns its attention to ethical hacking. The blog discusses penetration testing and computer security techniques that help you think like a hacker.

Uncommon Sense Security

Jack Daniel—and, no not the kind you imbibe in, is the leader and chief of Uncommon Sense Security. He updates the blog once a week with articles that focus on privacy and trust issues.

Stay Safe Online

The National Cyber-Security Alliance (NCSA) provides this resource for those wanting to stay in the know. They divide their postings into categories like mobile, social networking, and data privacy. Very informative and current.

Facecrooks.com

As you can tell by the title, this resource has everything to do with Facebook users. It's a wonderful way to stay up to date on Facebook's latest security threats. This resource will keep you informed about the latest scams and hoaxes that plaque Facebook.

Pauldotcom

Pauldotcom is Paul Asadoorian's weekly podcast called "Security Weekly." In it, Paul provides current news and technical segments and takes the tension off the topic by presenting it in a humorous way. His podcast is presented live every Thursday night at 6:00 p.m. EST.

Internet Storm Center

This resource gets the most traffic on the list, and it is perhaps the most well-known site in the bunch. Like CNN is to news, Internet Storm Center is to cyber security. It provides a constant stream of threat-related news.

CyberCrime & Doing Time

This program is led by Gary Warner. In it, Gary provides in-depth information about evolving threats, cybercrime, and legal issues regarding the security of your system. The great thing about Warner is that along with his highly educational information, he also offers step-by-step analysis of the latest threats, how to identify them, prevent them, and what to do if you should suffer an attack (26).

All these resources will help you and your employees to stay current with all that is happening in the hacker's world. Not only will you know some of the latest scams and hacks, but you'll also learn how to combat their effects. Burying your head in the sand is not an option. The best weapon, and sometimes the only weapon, you have to fight off hackers is to understand what motivates them and what they want to achieve from hacking your system. Only then can you protect your intellectual information and sensitive data.

Action is empowering—so, take action! Prepare yourself to win the battle against hackers, to arm yourself with the knowledge these resources can provide. You may not be able to get ahead of the hackers; even professional security companies have challenges where that is concerned. However, you can follow close behind and possibly prevent further fallout by reoccurring hacks.

Chapter 5: Conversation with a Hacker

As I was researching for this book, I came across one of the most interesting interchanges yet. It was a conversation between a blogger and the hacker who had contacted her to inform her of a system breach he had caused. Instead of offering a word-for-word account of the conversation, I have chosen segments that I believe will give you some insight into the mind of a hacker.

Blogger: "...why are you determined to hack the site?"

Hacker: "I'm gathering information. Because of my little attack, I've managed to find several new 0-day exploits. I'm just wanting to ... see how they patch the site, so I can see how I would need to find new 0-day exploits."

Blogger:	"Why so angry at them for blocking you...?"
Hacker:	"I wasn't mad; it was more of me having fun, lol."

Although this is highly unusual for someone to have a conversation with a hacker, it's that very thing that made this dialogue so fascinating. So, let's examine what the beginnings of this discussion tell us about the hacker. First, it doesn't sound like he is hacking for maliciousness or to utterly destroy the system. It rather looks like he is trying to learn more, to perfect his hacking capabilities. His hacking has led him to make some new discoveries, and that pleases him.

Of course, he doesn't think much about what it might be doing to the users. This is typical of the hacker. If getting what they want requires damage to others—oh well. Most of the time, hackers are cavalier with the feelings of others, the losses they cause. After all, they don't have to experience those first hand. They are gone when the chaotic aftermath of an attack is suffered. No matter the damage, the hacker rarely has to answer directly to the people who had to pay the price for his "fun."

This hacker is making a game of his attack. We do get an idea of the casual, selfish way he talks about his activities, with little regard for the user. In an earlier exchange that is not shown here, it is evident that the blogger is surprised that the hacker has revealed himself by contacting her to tell her of his exploits. However, these feelings are not returned by the hacker. He is not surprised that the blogger wishes to begin this conversation with him. He is a bit self-consumed with his 0-day achievements and tends to assume that the blogger is impressed with his work as well.

This is consistent with the typical character traits of the hacker. Self-centered—more focused on the challenges he has overcome in his hack than the probability that he has caused trouble for others.

When the hacker refers to 0-day, that is the term we discussed earlier called "zero day," which is malware that offers no time for the user to discover the hack. It just happens. So, he was manipulating the victim's system to explore ways to exploit others for the purpose of honing his hacking skills. Again, a rather self-serving attitude.

As the blogger continues the conversation, we hear the curiosity in her voice, as I believe the hacker must have heard as well. The hacker wasn't angry with the conversation; in fact, it seemed as though he was pleased that someone found value in what he had to say. At this point, the hacker says he's not angry—just having some fun. Not that this is the case with all hackers or even the majority of hackers, but with this particular one—it seems as though his intent is more to gather information than to cause harm or permanent damage. Although, in his attempts to get what he wants, the damage is done.

Blogger: "...why did you target
_____?"

Hacker: "It wasn't a target...These are
public scripts; people pay top-
dollar for exploits. So, I'm just
taking out what's easier. Then I
will go after a harder site next.
Nothing but business
and...knowledge."

Blogger: "...so you're doing it for money and
knowledge?"

Hacker: "Yes. If I see they don't have what I
want, I'll show them where the
vulnerability is. Someone with
good IT training can find and patch
it in mere seconds.

Now we discover the hacker's motives. He wants
to make some money by selling his knowledge or
services. Also atypical for a hacker, he is not
only willing to reveal himself to the blogger, but
he volunteers to show her where the

vulnerabilities are in her system. His last line in this segment of dialogue reinforces what we've been discussing in past chapters. Even the hacker knows how important it is to have good security or IT people who can locate and fix issues before they become bigger-than-life problems. So, good advice.

Blogger: "...would you charge them for this patch?"

Hacker: "...I would charge them but what's the point? Who knows; maybe I will just give the information for free and ask...to be a part of the #Security team. But, that's if I don't wanna be evil. Muahahaha. I'm just going to leave them alone."

To delve a little further into the hacker's mind, we see that perhaps he is educating himself for a future position with a security company or a future with the darker side of hackers. That's one thing about hackers—they know their value to the world of security. Many of the best security companies have hired professional hackers to break codes and recognize malware placed by hackers of the dark side. This hacker again verifies to the blogger that he doesn't wish to be evil. He even shows his sense of humor.

This hacker seems to be a bit more extroverted than some, showing his personality and a friendlier side of himself. Then he attempts to set the bloggers mind at ease, telling her he's just going to leave them alone. One would assume this hacker is young and hasn't been at his career too long. In most cases, the longer one hacks, the darker they become.

Blogger: "...Can you DM me an email address where I can shoot you some more questions?"

Hacker: "No problem. I'm not an evil person; I just like to expand my knowledge any way possible. I will even tell you a secret. I'm a ... teenager."

Now the hacker has done the unthinkable. He's revealed personal information about himself. This is something an experienced hacker would never do. In fact, they would go to any lengths to hide their presence and identity. Again, the hacker tries to reassure the blogger, telling her that he is not evil. He justifies his behavior, which I'm sure many Black Hat hackers do as they rob others of their identities or steal from their companies.

This hacker states, however, that he just wants to hone his skills. It's interesting how the hacker then confides in the blogger, telling her a secret. The love of secrets is pretty typical for a hacker. They live in a secret world and enjoy sneaking in and out of other's lives, cloaked in deception. The hacker continues with...

Hacker: "I'm a very young hacker...I've been into the scene for almost two years now. This is just a new alias since I pissed off a few .gov websites."

Okay, now the hacker has confirmed he is relatively new at the game of hacking. As inexperienced as he is, the hacker has already managed to anger some influential people on some government sites. He may not be as innocent as he appears. It doesn't take long for an innocent hacker to be influenced by the monetary promises of going deep.

Blogger: "Why did you disclose on Twitter that you had defaced the site and hacked into the DB? Wouldn't it have been better to stay quiet about it 'til you got the results you desired?"

Hacker: "I had the site defaced for almost two months. I've grown tired from the lack of security, so I had to make it public."

This shows us that even a novice or young hacker can sit undetected in a site for months. You would think that his youth made him impatient, but I believe hackers are impatient voyeurs by nature, eager to see the results of their interferences. He's bored of this game and ready to move on to the next exploit. What he says though is that he tires of their lack of security, which shows us that he is no longer challenged. That is one of the major rewards for a hacker, overcoming the challenges and the excitement of possibly being detected. When the game becomes mundane, most hackers move on to bigger and better things.

When asked what an ordinary developer can do to protect their sites from being hacked, the hacker offers these suggestions.

- The developer needs to know what he's doing.
- Templates are good if the developer looked through the source. Even the smallest file can lead to a backdoor or exploit.
- Don't trust third-party sources.
- Never use nulled software. Keep up with the stats for the site.

As the conversation continues, the hacker again points out the need for security.

Hacker: "_____ deserved this. Because of the lack of security, site information got leaked. They had a chance to protect all the users, but they didn't keep up in #Security. Every web designer or publisher should perform updates to stop things like this. As a coder, I'm sure you must agree somewhat."

Blogger: "I agree. It's important to keep your software updated and secure.

Hacker: "Now you see the reason for the public attack."

Now the hacker is showing some of his darker self. He has a need to teach a lesson to those who are not doing their job correctly, according to his expectations. He is beginning to show his feelings of superiority. The hacker cannot resist teaching a lesson, especially if he feels those who have developed the system or who own the system deserve what is coming. To most hackers, ignorance is deserving of trouble, and it is up to him to wield the punishment.

Blogger: "What would your response be to someone who referred to you as a script kiddie?"

Hacker: "I'd prove my knowledge. I hate when people call me that. I'm a hacker who tries his best to fight for his own goals."

Now we see into the mind of the hacker. Like most other hackers, he feels as though he has something to prove. He is fighting for a cause, even if the cause is personal. The blogger struck a nerve when she labeled the hacker a script kiddie. The most dangerous hackers are those who feel as though they have something to prove—that's when they seek revenge over those who refuse to recognize their power and skills. If the situation had been different, we might have witnessed this hacker do something vengeful to the blogger just to prove his capabilities. End of conversation!

Hacker: "If they meet a hacker and become friends, just make sure of one thing: NEVER TRUST THE DOWNLOADS (27)!"

This last bit of advice is so telling about the character of a hacker. Even if you call the hacker your friend, you can never entirely trust him.

We have had a glimpse inside the mind of a young, somewhat untainted hacker. Now let's have an inside look at a notorious "Black Hat" hacker named Black Dragon.

The Story of a Black Hat Hacker— Matthew Beddoes

In 2013, Matthew Beddoes (alias Black Dragon) was incarcerated for attempting to steal £6.5 million worth of carbon credits from the United Nations' computer system. Beddoes wasn't always criminally minded. He first became interested in the computer at the ripe old age of 5 years old. Beddoes spent most of his spare time on his Commodore 64 in the early years, but as he got into secondary school, he progressed to a PC.

From gaming on his Commodore 64, Beddoes graduated to exploring databases, Microsoft Word types of software and then moved to basic programming. Like many other hackers, Matthew Beddoes was self-taught. With a hacker's eagerness and his or her need to overcome continuous challenges, it's difficult for computer science courses of study to keep up with the ever-changing world of technology. For this reason, many outstanding hackers are self-taught, and yet they could teach the computer courses better than the professors. Hackers know this, and it's just one more thing that feeds their egos.

We regress, though. Let's return to our story. As a young teenager, Beddoes was already programming and hacking sites to see if he could obtain passwords. More times than not, he not only stole the passwords, but he did so quite quickly.   From there Beddoes progressed to viewing data contained in the company files of the systems he hacked.

Seeing sensitive information was much more fun than just trying to see if he could get passwords. In the beginning, Beddoes wasn't doing anything malicious with the passwords or the files; he was just snooping and having fun. He would challenge himself to see if he could locate the company's vulnerabilities. When he found them, he would frequently inform the business of their holes. He thought they should appreciate the information. After all, he just wanted to help them out.

Beddoes was surprised by the company's reaction to his discoveries. They blew him off. Who did he think he was? Who was this 16-year-old punk telling them how to protect their computer systems? Beddoes admitted much later if the companies he hacked had merely taken his information and thanked him for freely giving it, things might have gone differently for him. Instead, he felt unappreciated and emotionally abused. These are the feelings of many Black Hat hackers who move to the dark side.

Instead of being appreciated for his skillfully gained information, Beddoes was blown off. IT staffs didn't want their vulnerabilities to be exposed for fear the boss would think they weren't doing their jobs. Managers took it personally as if he was criticizing them. Beddoes felt totally unappreciated; nobody wanted to hear the truth, so he took his information elsewhere.

At first, he joined public hacker forums that were readily available. There he found other hackers—finally, people with whom he had a common interest. As he got better at his craft and spoke of his achievements, he was invited into forums that were not so accessible. These were where the Black Hat hackers roamed. They weren't there to make friends but to trade information and see if they could exploit one another. Observing those communicating in the forums presented a whole new challenge. He could learn a lot, so he watched and waited. It was like hacking the hackers.

Many years later, after Beddoes was released from prison, he was interviewed and asked what he thought about Black Hat hackers. Here's what he had to say.

The negativity I saw ten years ago has just escalated from there.
In today's world, Black Hats are all about ripping each other off—
about flame wars and trolling. It's counterproductive if you ask me.

However, back then as a new Black Hat hacker, Beddoes was learning how to make lots of money in the underworld of hackers. He pulled several heists that paid tidy sums. He stole 144,000 credit cards from a laptop shop, using them to make even more money. Beddoes didn't consider the consequences—what would happen to him if he got caught. He was living large, making incredible money doing what he loved to do—hack.

That's exactly what happened. In 2013, Matthew Beddoes woke up to 30 police officers surrounding his home. The Black Dragon was arrested for attempting to steal from the United Nations' computer system. He served his time and transformed himself from hacker to security specialist. He has now formed Red Dragon Security, but he admits to missing the freedom and excitement of the hacker's world (28).

The Hacker's Drug of Choice

The hacker's drug of choice has almost always been the thrill of the game, the challenge of the chase, and the feelings of superiority that is felt when they take someone down who previously wronged them. Like a drug, the hacker's vices demand more and more from its users. When the thrill of one discovery grows tiresome, the hacker moves on to hunt bigger game. That's when the Black Hat appeals to the fledgling wannabe, convincing him or her that the companies that were destroyed or those that lost all their data got what was coming to them.

It never hurts that the money to be made in Black Hat hacking is over-the-top, either. We're talking into the millions for the real experts. Black Hats don't have to pay student loans, apply for jobs, or go to the boss for a raise. They continue to make millions, but it isn't long before all is lost to even the best of hackers. Soon the drug rules—hacking rules the hacker. They become less and less satisfied with their ability to defy the odds, and that's when they begin to take greater risks with the predictable outcome of someday getting caught. The strange thing is that most hackers don't every consider the consequences of being trapped by a game of their own choosing. They don't think about the drug of hacking stealing from them as well—robbing them of a normal life and a satisfying future.

These highly intelligent individuals could have become owners, executives, or high-ranking officials, but instead, they just kept seeking greater hacking challenges that required more risks with monetary rewards that they believed warranted the work. Ask any reformed Black Hat hacker if they miss being a part of the underworld of hackers, and almost 100 percent of them will admit to feeling a void. It's not the friends they miss because hackers at this level don't make many friends. It's the danger, the excitement, and the ongoing challenge of doing it better than everyone else.

I believe many hackers are egotists. They're not loud and obnoxious about their feelings of superiority. They just feel it within themselves every time they hide malware inside someone's system and watch files disappear. They get a thrill out of capturing hundreds of passwords and credit card numbers, knowing it took them much less time than another talented hacker. The childish games of long ago have turned into a high-stakes effort with limitless financial rewards. There is something in a hacker's life that sounds a little attractive to all of us, don't you think?

Hackers can work from home without the boss leaning over their shoulder making unreasonable demands. Hackers of the criminal sort can write their own check when it comes to the amount of money to be had as a Black Hat hacker. Good hackers are admired by their fellow hackers, notorious for their outstanding skills. They have a reputation to uphold.

Hackers are praised for their skills, talent, and knowledge, much like a celebrity. However, they don't have to suffer the exposure of the rich and famous. They can remain a shadow under a mountain of success. They don't pay taxes on their gains, don't worry about what the market is doing unless they are hacking Wall Street, and they don't have a heavy capital investment to get their business going. It's built over a period of years.

Hackers also don't have to worry about employees, payroll, management, or inventory. Their primary asset is their mind, and their tools are all the tricks of the hacker's trade. There is one thing they must concern themselves with, however. It is another hacker. They never trust. Isn't that a lonely existence? Nobody to share your successes with, and nobody to inquire about the difficulties you might experience as you conduct another hack. Many of them don't even share with their families where they go at night, tucked in the dark recesses of their computers. They just hack all alone in their home office or the basement.

There is no public recognition or awards for Black Hat hacker of the year, and no congratulations for designing the malware of the month. When it's been a particularly stressful day, it's not like the Black Hat hacker goes online and commiserates with his peers. Instead, tomorrow is much like today. It's a constant quest for excellence in an industry that will never recognize its peak performers. Black Hat hackers don't talk about their day with their spouses as they sit at the dining room table. I couldn't say for sure, but I would guess many of them work through their sandwich and chips alone at their desks while trolling for their next victim.

The computer is the hacker's mistress, and she's a demanding one. The strongest relationship the hacker has is the one he builds with his networks, treating each newest conquest like the birth of a child. What starts out being a proud moment, ends up keeping you up at night and demanding more of your time than you care to give. Soon, you turn into this one-dimensional person when you hack in the same league as the Black Hats. You lose your human identity and become a computer creature with a name that defines your underworld behavior.

The more people call you by your hacker's name, the less you remember what it was like to be the real you. On the street, when people call you by your given name, you fail to respond. You don't think of yourself as Paul or Amy any longer; now you are Poison and Alamon. When the transformation is complete, your brain becomes more and more like a calculating computer. Gone is your compassion and loyalty, lost in the coding of a hacker's hell.

It sounds dramatic, I know, and that's because a Black Hat hacker has lost his soul. The computer has gobbled up his potential and robbed him of real joy. It is quite a dramatic metamorphosis, but one that isn't evidenced by one's outside appearance. All the changes, all the losses are internal, just as those experienced at the hands of a hacker.

Perhaps there is more to learn from the Black Hat hacker, and that is a lesson in how to hide your feelings and cope with the loss of oneself. As much as hackers love their life as a hacker, it's a short-lived preoccupation. Black Hat hackers began their careers young, but they end them young as well. Many are arrested, recruited by security companies, or give up their drug cold turkey. Once they do, it's a day-by-day fight to stay away from the drug.

What begins as a game to win, soon becomes a game of survival. Suddenly, the rules change and no matter how much hackers consider themselves to be nonconformists, they are forced to play by the rules or get out of the game. Many things are unacceptable, things they are not permitted to do and still belong to the Black Hat group. They cannot befriend others. They cannot reveal their identity. They cannot tolerate computer ignorance. They cannot ever look at the outside of a computer program without wanting to move inside to partake of that beloved underworld drug—the hack.

Chapter 6: Hiring a Black Hat

For all its seduction, the Dark Web cannot always contain or control the top-notch hackers. Black Hat hackers whose talents are well-known in the underworld of criminal hackers are often swayed to go legitimate. It isn't always the temptation of more money. The mature mind of a hacker who has decided to listen to his good sense after years of hiding and usually some prison time, just might prevail. A hacker's world seems to be constantly evolving—from playful, mischievous kid to criminal young adult, and finally to a more mature adult seeking the real-life rewards of a legal career.

In fact, many hackers end up working for the very companies they have successfully and creatively hacked. The more challenging the hack, the more likely they will be recognized for their abilities to do the seemingly impossible. Perhaps that's the dream of many Black Hat hackers—to be offered a legit career in the government or with the companies they previously persecuted.

It's incredible what these hackers can do above ground in legitimate firms. Not only are they able to develop programs and write code that is undeniably superior, but they know how the minds of Black Hat hackers work. What an advantage they have, and so do the corporations who hire them. At least they can rest assured they won't be victimized with their employee's hacks anymore. Or, can they?

Curious as to what makes Black Hat hackers turn White Hat, we decided to follow several hackers who have made that successful transition. As the research shows, there are some traits of a Black Hat hacker that are never whitewashed. They are usually still risk takers, but now those risks are more calculated and controlled—specific to their assigned jobs. They are still nonconformists, but they have learned to adapt their experiences and skills to a standardized corporate or government expectation.

Not only have the hackers learned, but so too have the entities who hire former Black Hat hackers. Clearly, they understand that these employees or consultants are a different breed of developer and programmer. Their minds see what others don't, and that's what gives them value to corporations. Plus, they have honed their skills, made computers their entire world for most of their lives, so that curious spark and need to be challenged must be kept alive. For hackers, what appeals to them will never be the nine to five, dress to impress, corporate "yes" geek. Not the Black Hats of this world!

Hackers of the Black Hat variety will always question a company's methods and policy; that's what makes them tick. The problem is when hiring these "outside the box" thinkers, employers then attempt to make the Black Hats fit into a world that is entirely foreign to them. In truth, the value of a Black Hat hacker lays with his or her ability to be comfortable in that "one-step-out" position. So, if you are considering convincing a hacker from the underworld to join your corporate team, know that the traits you most value in their performance will also be the ones that make you the craziest. They'll be impossibly independent, working late at night and showing up far past an acceptable hour in the morning. Just about the time you consider having the "talk" with them about performance, they will surprise you with something off the radar brilliant. They absolutely cannot and will not be micro-managed, preferring not to discuss their current project until they have a breakthrough in development. They are impatient with useless meetings, listening to people they often consider to be rather useless people.

You might also have issues with other workers who find the new Black Hat aloof and distant when invited to be on certain committees or participate in group activities. It's almost certain; the Black Hat will not be in attendance at these events. They won't make excuses or apologize; they just won't be there. In fact, consider yourself lucky if you even get a reply. Black Hats reserve conversations for computers; the Black Hat rarely moves away from their desk or climbs outside their screens to discuss the mundane.

If you are a company or government agency, and still interested in hiring a reformed Black Hat, the following are a list of possible conflicts you may experience.

Potential Conflicts When Hiring a Reformed Black Hat Hacker

We've mentioned a few issues to consider when hiring a previous Black Hat hacker, but here's a more extensive list to review.

- If your clients know their personal information is in the hands of a criminal, they may have issues with using your services. If you are a security company, you might have a difficult job trying to persuade clients to give you their personal information. Most will question whether you can protect them against the very type of hacker you just hired. So, keeping the hired hacker out the limelight is to your advantage. This shouldn't be too challenging since most reformed Black Hat hackers don't want to deal with the public anyway.

- If your company deals with government contracts that require a security clearance, they might have issues with a known criminal in your employee. At the least, an explanation may be to gain the client's trust and confidence. If you vouch for the reformed Black Hat, you'll be putting your reputation on the line.

- Of course, the question in most employers' minds is whether the Black Hat has turned White Hat, or simply gone gray—sometimes delving into the same criminal behaviors of their shady past. If you have your doubts, what do you do? Do you allow the Black Hat to have access to your confidential files? It's all about trust, and you have a right to be weary of his or her activities.

- Black Hat hackers are masters at manipulation. If you enter into an employment agreement with one, watch that you aren't being manipulated by a hacker that hasn't reformed after all. You certainly don't want to become their next challenge. If the hacker turns on you, the only ones who stands to benefit from the arrangement are probably your competitors.

- You could also be opening you and your company up to lawsuits should your business's security be breached. Think of the ramifications of hiring a known criminal who previously made a career out of stealing confidential information, and yet you purposefully put your clients in harm's way. The only thing that would cost you more than putting your company back together again after the Black Hat was done with you would be the astronomical legal fees to follow.

- Then you must consider whether the hacker is as good as he says he is. It's not as if they come with shining references or a resume that publicly touts their achievements. All you have to go on is what you have discovered about their work. The question is, were they script kiddies who previously ripped off other hackers; or, did they do the programming themselves? It would be too bad to have taken all these chances with your files, only to discover that the hacker isn't what they represented themselves to be.

- Then, of course, what if the time comes that you have to let the hacker go? Will he hack your files as payback? Will you ever really feel safe again once the Black Hat has entered your domain?

- Black Hat hackers belong to a very elite group of hackers. They sometimes brag about their exploits, malware, backdoors, worms, virus attacks, and all other tricks they may have up their sleeves. Even reformed Black Hat hackers will have trouble keeping their distance from long-time hacker friends who are as good if not better than they are. Will you have to worry that the hacker you hire will accidentally talk about your company's secrets? Perhaps!

- If you haven't been scared off yet, keep reading. One of the things that should be a must on your list of issues to overcome is to research your hacker before hiring. If he has never been arrested, it might be difficult to know his particular Achilles heel, when it comes to what might tempt him in the future. For example, if your hacker hates government regulations and conformities, and your company deals with a lot of government contracts, this hacker is probably not the one for you. With the mindset of mistrust for governmental agencies, it will most likely be impossible for him to turn off the hate for your political clients.

- Black Hat hackers are used to having no boundaries, so you'll have to be aware of how they handle your expectations. Don't give the hacker full access to your data until you have worked together long enough to build a trusting relationship. Show them "no mercy" when it comes to breaking the rules. If they break the rules or your company policies in one area, they are most likely doing so in other areas. If you catch them in an act that goes against your policy, cut them loose. This employment agreement must offer no second chances.

- Since hiring the Black Hat will put you and your company at a much higher risk, you'll need to communicate that to your insurance company. You wouldn't want to hide the fact that you have a hacker and then find out too late your insurance won't cover your losses. In addition to the standard insurance, it might be a good idea for you to make sure this particular employee is bonded.

- When it's time for you and the Black Hat to part ways, make sure to change all your passwords. Taking active preventative measures to detect any malware or other intrusive devices that could be placed in your software would also be critical.

After having examined all the negative issues, there are some incredible things that a reformed Black Hat hacker can do like no other. Black Hats have experience on handling the offensive side of the security business. They know how hackers think, and they enjoy the game. Whereas, your IT experts have most always been on the defense, spending most of their time one step outside the circle. Those of you who are football fans know there's a big difference between your offensive and defensive teams.

It's like looking through a window from opposite sides. The defense is always looking out, trying to identify who could be out there lurking in the shadows, and what they might be planning next. Those on the offense, the hackers, are playing and enjoying the street games, trying to come up with the next most impressive play. To the defensive IT professional, computer security is a job or a career. To the offensive hacker, this is a high-stakes game that he needs to manipulate and control (29).

What If You're an Individual with a Need to Hire a Hacker?

Although we've discussed the issues and potential problems of a corporation or government hiring a hacker, what about the individual who just has a particular job or project they want to be done? Sure, it may be illegal, but your need outweighs your fears—for the moment! How would you go about doing that? It's not like you can search the classifieds for a hacker to steal passwords or hack a few accounts for you, right?

First of all, similar to the companies that hire hackers, you can suffer losses as well. Before you hire a hacker, know that you are playing with fire. You know what happens to most people who play with fire? Yep! They get burned! Don't close your eyes to the possibilities.

So, you still want to hire a hacker, huh? Okay, where do you go from here? Like everything else, it depends on what you want to be done and what level of skills your hacker will need to possess. If your hack needs are above board, the first thing to do is search online and enter something like hiring a hacker. You'll soon be shopping a lot of White Hat hackers who are happy to help for the right price. It won't be difficult to find the right hacker; there are plenty to choose from who can easily fulfill your request.

Now let's get to where most of you who are needing to hire a hacker are coming from—you want an unscrupulous hacker, one that has no problem cracking some databases, email accounts, or messing with somebody's computer or phone. Okay, now we're talking a whole other level of need. We put it nicely when we said you wanted an unscrupulous hacker, because what you're looking for is a criminal. So that you realize, hiring a criminal to perform a criminal act makes you a criminal as well.

Just as the corporations take a chance hiring reformed Black Hats, you also put yourself out there. In fact, your risk is even higher because you are not looking for a reformed hacker, your search is for the known culprit who's willing to sell themselves for the almighty dollar. A mercenary hacker, if you will. Your set of problems is much different from those hiring a "so-called" reformed specialist.

There are sites where you can shop for these types of hackers as well. Two of the most well-known and popular sites are Hire 2 Hack and HireHacker. They typically address requests like stealing databases, hijacking websites and Facebook accounts, and discovering passwords. One of the sites for hire that was viewed by a New York Times reporter was said to have over 6,000 job requests, averaging $200 to $300 per hack (30).

There are three initial problems to consider when hiring a Black Hat hacker, and if you fail to go in with your eyes wide open, you are setting yourself up for a host of other problems in which you'll wish you'd never been exposed.

Three Primary Problems When Individuals Hire a Black Hat

Other than the obvious, that your hired gun might turn on you and hack your system, it will pay you to be aware of these three things.

1. You have absolutely no leverage when hiring a hacker. There is no way you can hold a criminal accountable. Who are you going to call if they take your money and run? Who are you going to report them to if they screw you over? It's not like you can walk into a police station and report the criminal you hired to the authorities. I can hear you now saying, *"Well, I won't pay them until the job's complete. If they don't do what I want, I won't pay them at all."* Oh, yea! Good luck with that. Now you have exposed all your personal information and pissed off a powerful hacker. Not a good combination.

2. Because you know nothing about what they do, how are you going to verify whether they did a good job or not? Sure, you have your information, but what if their activities can be traced back to you? Now you're an accomplice. In most states, you are just as guilty as the hacker you

hired. Also, what if the hacker decides you have deep pockets and attempts to blackmail you? You could be paying for your foolish act for years to come. Or, your information along with your request could be the one exposed to the public. Is that something in which you are prepared to handle?

3. How are you going to pay for the requested job? This may sound minor, but you certainly don't want to pay by credit card, right? If you pay by PayPal, the hacker can hack into your account. Before hiring the hacker, find out if there is any secure currency that can be used so that you can be assured of no future bank hacks. Some have suggested Bitcoin, which is a person to person transaction that allows payment of currency that can be used by the recipient to purchase in places that accept Bitcoin. Perhaps you agree to pay in product or purchasing

power on eBay. If you deposit money into the hacker's PayPal account, make sure it's done in a way that cannot be traced.

Another problem that can be disconcerting is the fact that once you are in the company of Black Hat hackers, you're surrounded by others criminals of equal or greater danger than the one you hired. The difference between Black Hat hackers and White and Gray Hat hackers is that Black Hats are much more likely to hack one another. If your hacker is on a forum, bragging about the job he did for you, indicating that you paid way too much, there's a good chance several other Black Hats are going to pay your computer a visit.

Months later, just about the time you are congratulating yourself for having pulled off a hack with no backlash, you'll notice one evening that your computer is not performing quite right. Or, your Facebook page has been defaced. Or, the balances in your bank account are surprisingly low. Welcome to the hackers'

173

roundtable. Be assured of one thing. If hackers do a hack job FOR you, they'll do a hack job TO you. It could be just a matter of time before you learn this lesson the hard way.

I'm sure you've heard when contemplating doing something illegal that it's never too late to change your mind. It's an option that many have used just before they are about to do something stupid. Instead of committing armed robbery, the criminal walks on by the liquor store and tucks the gun back in his pocket. Even if he has entered the premises, he can choose to walk around and then leave. It wasn't too late to change his mind about committing a felony and taking the chance of being caught.

I wish we could apply that same thinking to hiring a hacker. Once you have tapped into a site of hungry hackers—it's too late to change your mind. Sure, you can back out, but you may have already made all your information available to every hacker on the website. For this reason, if you're a little wishy-washy about whether or not you want to hire a hacker, stop and think about the consequences. If you just want to browse and shop a hacker for hire's website, do so on another computer that has been wiped clean of any valuable data and contacts.

If you are using a computer that is used for little else, make sure you are also using an old email that is not connected to your current one. Just like paper trails, computers leave traceable avenues that hackers can travel until they discover your information. Don't give hackers the opportunity to turn on you. If you're going to do business with a criminal, then you've got to learn to think like one.

Trust no one! Don't befriend a hacker thinking he or she would not betray you now that you have gotten to know one another. Wrong! Hackers manipulate and control—they hack. They have no sense of fair play. Everything is open to their hack if you have the right currency. When using your phone, make sure it cannot be traced back to your everyday computer that you want to be protected.

We've talked about hacking computers, but don't think your phone is safe. Your phone can be the next hit by an enterprising hacker. There are all kinds of spyware out that will let you quickly access text messages. These methods are so easy to use, even the novice can become an amateur hacker. Beware, though, once you enter the hacker's world, you might find an attraction to the beneath the surface behaviors of today's hacker.

Chapter 7: Notorious Black Hat Hackers

This chapter will be especially dedicated to notorious Black Hat and some Gray Hat hackers. They are not listed in any order of importance or influence. While their stories are interesting, their acts are often frightening and sad for us mere mortals who are unfamiliar with the words and ways of notorious hackers. Some have become almost legendary, and some will surprise you at their achievements, but they all have made the precarious journey from Black Hat hackers to somewhat legitimate developers and entrepreneurs.

These "so-called" reformed hackers have left a trail of damage in their rise to the top. In reading their stories, you be the judge whether their lives' works are genius accomplishments or juvenile attempts to become legendary hackers. Either way, these Black Hat hackers have turned

the computer science world on end with their
brilliance and boldness.

George Hotz—(alias geohot)

George is an intelligent, talented hacker with a
curious mind and an overactive imagination.
This is meant to be a compliment, as they are the
perfect traits for a hacker to possess. At just 17-
years-old George was the first person to carrier
unlock an iPhone. His talent was apparently
recognized by the founder of Certicell, Terry
Diadone, as well. It was reported that George
traded his second unlocked 8 GB iPhone to
Daidone for a Nissan 350Z and three 8 GB
iPhones. So, Hotz learned very early on that
hacking came with excellent fringe benefits.

Hotz didn't stop there. Shortly after his iPhone
hack, he focused his attention on the Sony
PlayStation 3. In 2010, Holz released his
discoveries to the public, showing everyone his
expertise in using a jailbreak tool and bootrom

exploit for iOS, which gave him read and write access to the PlayStation 3's system memory and CPU. Hotz was pushing the envelope with Sony, as he released at the 27th Chaos Communications Congress technical conference later that same year how he and his group, failOverflow, had penetrated the device's security model, which gave them the root signing and encryption keys.

It was Sony's turn to fight back, and so it did with a vengeance. By January 2011, Hotz found himself in another starring role, that of the defendant in a lawsuit between Sony and failOverflow, to be heard in the U.S. District Court of Northern California. The suit was settled out of court, with Hotz promising never again to hack into any Sony system or device.

Hotz's success as a hacker was known throughout the entire hacker universe, and it didn't take long for his achievements and skills to reach the ears of some of the biggest names in the legitimate arenas of Social Media and Website development. He worked with

Facebook and Google, but George's stint with these powerhouses was short-lived. Hotz's heart's desire was to create his company, and that's where you'll find him today. He's currently busy with comma.ai, working hard to develop vehicular automation technology to complement or perhaps rival Tesla's Autopilot.

Throughout the past nine or ten years, Hotz has received the lion's share of media attention regarding notorious hackers. He's been interviewed by the *Today Show*, Fox CNN, NBC, CBS, G4, ABC, CNBC, and featured in national magazines, newspapers, and websites from coast-to-coast. Growing a bit weary of all the media attention, George Hotz has dropped out of the public eye of late, choosing to focus all his attentions on his growing company, comma.ai (31). At just 26 years old now, we suspect you haven't heard the last of George Hotz.

Peter Hajas

After he had created his famous replacement notifications system for jailbroken iOS devices, Peter got the attention of a particular "fruit" company in the high-tech world of communications products and software, if you know what I mean. Hajas hack now allows iPhone users to use almost any apps instead of relying on Apple's exclusive built-in system. We don't have much early information on Hajas, only that he's one of Apple's newest interns (32).

Hiring Hajas to work at Apple as an intern has been kept on the down low, though. Who knows, perhaps Peter is so used to living beneath the surface of real-world activities that this is the way he prefers it. However notorious Hajas has become, Apple is treating him as any other intern, or are they? Obviously, Apple wasn't all that eager to run into him in the hacker's hall of fame, so they gave him a job in the Apple tower.

Jeff Moss—(alias Dark Tangent)

Jeff Moss was too young to drive or vote, but when he received his first computer at the age of 10, he was quite excited to learn he could interact with adults all over the world. From then on, Moss was hooked on computers. He graduated with a BA in Criminal Justice from Gonzaga University and worked for Ernst & Young, LLP in their information System Security division. From there Moss became a director at Secure Computing Corporation where he helped to establish the Professional Services Department in the U.S., Australia, and Asia.

Although Moss's education, credentials, and career references are impressive, he is most known for the creation of Black Hat Briefings computer security conference, which is an unusual gathering of information security experts from around the globe. He has since sold Black Hat for a whopping $13.9 million, at just 41 years old. What began as a talented hacking career has made Moss a multi-millionaire.

In 1993, Moss created the first DEF CON hacker convention, whose core members were the Fido hacking network out of Canada. We believe that is Moss's baby since DEF CON was not included in the Black Hat sale. Moss is the perfect example of hackers not being all about the money. Even though he's worth millions, he's still out there working to maintain the security of our government's computer systems.

Today, Moss works as a consultant for a Seattle-based security company. He's been consulted on concerns like the situation between U.S. and China regarding email threats and various system hacks (33). It's amazing to think that Jeff's one of the oldest Black Hat hackers, and he's just in his 40s.

Chris Putnam

Putnam is another example of being hired by the very company he so successfully hacked. It was in 2005 when Putnam threatened Facebook by creating a worm that made Facebook profiles look like MySpace ones. At the time, Facebook's COO, Dustin Moscovitz, discovered Putnam was behind the hack and was reported to have sent him a note that read something like this:

Hey, this was funny, but it looks like you are deleting contact information

from users' profiles when you go to replicate the worm again. That's

not so cool.

From their very first communication, it was evident Putnam and Moscovitz shared many commonalities, including a mutual respect and admiration for one another. The next thing Putnam knew; he was being invited by Facebook's Moscovitz to come in for an interview. Putnam didn't know what would be waiting for him as he entered Facebook's headquarters, heading for the 2nd floor where he would finally meet Dustin Moscovitz face-to-face. Well, that was his hope, anyway.

Putnam admitted that he feared Moscovitz wouldn't be the only one waiting for him as the elevator doors opened, but that the floor would be crowded with cops ready to make an arrest. But Moscovitz was alone and welcomed Putnam with a warm greeting and another joke. After the interview had gone on for a while, Moscovitz whispered to Putnam: *"It's just a really long con; the cops will be waiting for you!"*

Pleased to be working with such a great company, Putnam had this to say about Facebook. *"I will be forever grateful that the company was so sympathetic toward people like myself. It's one of the things that really sets Facebook apart with its passion for scrappy, hacker-type engineers* (34).*"*

Michael "Mikeyy" Mooney

At 17 years old, still attending high school in Brooklyn, Mikeyy coded a Twitter worm that sent tweets from hundreds of accounts to a spam website. Mikeyy's work caught the attention of Twitter's co-founder, Biz Stone, who was anxious about Mikeyy's advanced skills at such a young age, and vowed that he was going to press charges if all activities on Twitter didn't stop.

Stone wasn't the only one who was watching Mikeyy's hacking activities. Not long after his Twitter hack, Mikeyy received several job offers, of which he accepted a job as a developer with an Oregon-based web application developer—exqSoft Solutions (35). Like several other Black Hats, Michael's resume was his hack!

Johnny Chung Lee

Lee's claim to fame was his hack on Nintendo Wiimote in 2008. Amazingly, Lee was able to hack into their system with a ballpoint pen and infrared lights. When Microsoft recognized his true capabilities, even though they had been misdirected in the hack, they hired Lee to help them develop the Kinect. Lee was later named one of the world's top 35 innovators under 35.

In 2011, Google did a hack job of their own, stealing Lee from Microsoft to become a "rapid evaluator" on some of their innovative applications. It's difficult to tell who are the worst hackers, the companies who poach or the hackers themselves. Either way, when word gets out that these infamous hackers have signed up with a great corporation, another is right on their heels to poach their new found hacker talent. It's obvious that Lee didn't do much complaining, anticipating his new career with Google.

Kevin Poulsen

Kevin is famous for his hack into L.A.'s KIIS-FM radio station where he rigged a competition that won him a Porsche. Along with being motivated by monetary gains, Poulsen also created a program that identified hundreds of sex offenders on MySpace.

Like many other Black Hats, Poulsen went to the Dark Web, as he grew more and more bold, eventually breaching FBI computers. As a result, Poulsen was arrested in 1991. He served five long years in prison, paid a hefty fine of $56,000 for mail, wire, and computer fraud, and after his release found himself a young felon with no job and no plan for his future.

However, Poulsen knew what it was like to scratch his way to the top. He needed to search for something other than hacking, so he followed his desire to become a journalist and is now the senior editor at *Wired Magazine* (36).

Michael Calce—(alias MafiaBoy)

Calce didn't wait until adulthood to hit the big-time Black Hat hackers. As a daring 15-year-old, MafiaBoy did the unthinkable. With his hack, he shut down major websites, to include Dell, Amazon, Yahoo, CNN, eBay, and E-Trade. Calce was one of those hackers who was young and rash and had something to prove. One of his fellow hackers said that CNN.com's site could never be brought down because of its "advanced networks" and "huge traffic numbers." That was all it took to challenge Calce. The challenge of his co-hacker was what motivated Calce to achieve the impossible.

Calce hit CNN's server with so many requests that the server was unable to function properly, and Calce proudly admitted to slowing CNN down for nearly two hours. His attack on Yahoo was quite by accident. It seems that Calce had entered the IP addresses into the script and then went to school, forgetting to shut down his computer. When he came back to his house after school, he found his computer had crashed and later while listening to the news he discovered why. It was his abandoned and independent computer that was responsible for all the havoc being reported on the news, not Calce.

Calce has commented on many occasions that it is easier to launch attacks now than it was back in the day. Here it is, more than ten years after his reckless juvenile hacks, and yet companies are still completely unaware of the risks they are taking because they refuse to secure their systems. Although the companies have not progressed in their security measures, hackers have grown leaps and bounds in their hacking capabilities. The playing field is by far in the hacker's favor. There is hardly a day that goes by when you don't hear about another cyber crime being perpetrated on one of our top corporations or governmental agencies.

At Calce's peak, he and his fellow hackers were curiously running tests and attempting to infiltrate systems for the challenge and excitement success could bring. Today's hackers have much more sinister motivations for hacking. If it isn't for the money, today's hackers are out to damage and destroy. With monetary gain becoming the hacker's mindset, it is much more likely that wealthy individuals will be targeted as much as businesses.

Michael Calce leaves us with these words of wisdom: *"Users should beware of open wireless networks because it is incredibly easy to eavesdrop on what you are doing. People don't realize this* (37).

Since we know hacking will never go away, and mercenary hackers are here to stay, it's up to each one of us to take the appropriate measures to secure out home and business systems. Crying after the fact, or should I say after the hack, isn't going to bring back your computer, phone, accounts, money, or identity. We haven't discussed the possibilities of identity theft so far, and there's a reason for that. Contrary to what most people believe, identity theft makes up only a small part of the hacker's portfolio of accomplishments.

Part of the reason many hackers don't mess with stealing someone else's identity is that it's just so easily accomplished there's no challenge. There is no reward for the hacker, no bragging rights on having accomplished the hack. In fact, most of the time nobody knows what or who caused their identities to be stolen. Hackers have reported that stealing one's identity is so easy that a novice computer user can be taught to do so within a matter of minutes. Most of the time, identities are taken because of a person's carelessness not a hacker's skills.

Come to think of it; that could probably be said about all stolen information. If not for our lack of security and our careless and casual use of passwords, a hacker's job would be much more challenging. The responsibility of protecting our data is in our hands. It is up to the user to discourage a hack attack. Now that you have been exposed to the many things you can do to deter attacks, you have flat run out of excuses.

What's the Common Denominator?

It's a legitimate question. What is common to all the hacks we have discussed? Or should I say WHO is the common denominator? It's you and me—the unsuspecting public. A hacker cannot steal, if there is no available information or data. A hacker will probably move on if we haven't been lazy if we frequently update our systems and take measures to protect ourselves. The commonalities of most hacks is that their damage could have been minimized or prevented altogether if we, the public, had done our job as well.

It's useless for us to continually blame our losses on hackers alone. There are always going to be hackers, and victims, but doing our share will help to keep the hackers at bay. The things that hackers don't want you to know is that their power doesn't begin and end with a computer. If their aim is to control, then anything that we open to them to control, will result in our loss. Once again, we are the common denominator.

Unfortunately, another common denominator for Black Hat hackers is that most don't escape detection nor the legal ramifications of their illegal activities. Just about the time most teens are choosing which college to attend and having a great time dating, the young Black Hat hacker is experiencing restless nights trying to stay one step ahead of the law. Many who have been caught served years in prison when they were in their early 20s.

As victims, we may suffer losses of equipment, sometimes a great deal of money, and our privacy. The Black Hat hacker loses his or her freedom. Many don't see the consequences clearly; they're just young kids who let their talent and curiosity run away with them. They wrap themselves in a cocoon of false security that reassures them they'll never be caught. Because they can hide behind their computers and snoop for years without detection, they believe they'll escape prison as well. When that is not the case, they carry with them for the rest of their lives all that they suffered there. While the rest of us experience our loss and move on, the time spent in prison places scars on the hackers' minds that cannot be removed.

It is my opinion that most Black Hat hackers don't consciously choose the Dark side, it chooses them. Just as they got sucked into the life of hacking, they too gradually lose their ability to reason like ordinary people. Their reasoning gets clouded along the way by their desire to continue to play the game, to move through a world of deception that taints them somehow. Because their activities with others who don't hack are limited, all they are exposed to are criminally-minded individuals whose mental processes and emotional makeup limit their insight. Another common denominator— limited insight into real-world consequences for their hacking behaviors.

Most hackers believe that they are the exception to the rule. They'll never go to jail, even if they continue to do illegal things. Instead, they'll be rewarded just like the gentlemen we spoke of earlier. It happens to all good hackers, right? They'll pull off an amazing hack and will be rewarded by being offered a job with a huge corporation. They picture themselves finally walking into a boardroom of admiring executives who give them the keys to the kingdom because of their exceptional talent.

It's a pipedream! The vast majority of hackers remain small time hackers whose hobby is snooping into the lives of others. They don't discover incredible malware that will enable them to secretly rule the world. Instead, they mature into rather lonely, isolated adults with few emotional attachments. If it cannot be plugged in or doesn't need to be charged, it most likely won't carry much meaning in their lives.

Another common denominator is that most hackers, especially those who consider themselves to be hacking for a greater cause, don't think they are doing anything wrong. If they hack to spy and snoop but don't do any real damage, what's the harm, right? In fact, the "hacktivist" believes they are doing good when they expose a government or political figure whom they have judged guilty by public exposure. It is somehow the hacker's right to decide who suffers and who escapes public humiliation. Consequently, in a way, the common denominator for many hackers is that they have a twisted sense of judgment.

Hackers live in a virtual world where rewards and power are given to those who take. Over time, the superior feelings and inflated egos of many hackers lead them to believe their rightful place is to set in judgment of us other underlings. We are not to question their decisions, but merely to suffer our designated punishment and learn to change our ways. Of course, we're speaking in the extremes. Many hackers have fun at the expense of others, and we never know about it. We're the joke in their criminal games, but we're unaware of what's going on behind the screens of our computers. Like the hackers, we find ourselves living in the dark.

Chapter 8: Tools of the Trade

Every worthy hacker utilizes tools of the trade to improve their skills and communicate with the public in a language that we typically cannot understand or are not interested enough to learn. Most of us regular users operate on a "need-to-know" basis. We don't have an all-consuming desire to know how something works; we just want to know it will work when we need it.

The thinking of a hacker is much different. They, on the other hand, have a deep need to know how things work so they can then turn around and make them not work. Sounds like a circular explanation, but hackers tear down and reconstruct all the time. To communicate what they do, they have created a whole new computer language. For fear of causing systems overload, we tried to avoid throwing too many terms at you in the very beginning. However, now that you are somewhat knowledgeable about the way hackers think and the methods they employ, we decided to provide you with a working dictionary of hacker terminology.

Knowing what these terms mean are the first things that should be included in your hacker toolbox. The hackers' language is their most necessary tools of the trade. Because they navigate in a different world, the terms they use to describe their journey are words the average user has heard about but can't quite define. So, let's define them for you.

The Hackers Glossary of Terms

Even if you're not a newbie hacker and you believe hacking does not affect your life, these terms will go a long way to help you understand where not to go on your searches and what not to do should you go there by mistake. You will probably be surprised how many of these terms sound familiar, but you never knew before what they meant.

Adware

You've probably noticed all the little ads that surround the topics you browse on the web. However, have you also noticed how those ads seem to be all about your interests? For example, if you consistently browse sites featuring the latest and greatest power tools, you'll soon be noticed how many popup ads or ads that complement your browsing habits will be about power tools. That might be because of adware.

Adware is a form of spyware used to track your browsing habits without your knowing and then generate related ads. We've warned you before about clicking on some of these ads, but it's worth a rewrite. Some of the ads you'll see popping up on sites you visit are coded with malware. Resist the click.

Back Door

Back doors are exactly what they sound like. They are a way for hackers to enter into computers or other devices without being detected. By creating a back door, hackers can bypass security measures we typically use like logins and passwords. Hackers have designed malware to exploit back doors that have been intentionally placed there by government intelligence on its more sophisticated programs.

Bot

Bots are programs that are used to automate an action to allow it to be repeated at a much higher rate for a longer period of time than humans could achieve. Outside the hackers' world, bots are used quite legitimately for online content delivery. However, when hackers use them they often use them to generate calls that create denial of service attacks.

Botnet

Botnet is a group of hijacked computers used to send spam or make denial of service attacks. They send directives through these "zombie" computers, sending spam messages through an extended network.

Burp Suite

This is an integrated platform that allows security testing on web apps. Burp Suites tools support the entire testing process to enable hackers to exploit system vulnerabilities.

Compiler

Compilers are programs used to translate a hackers' high-tech language into language the machine can understand. Compilers are often written to create backdoors and avoid changing the programs initial code.

DoS (Denial of Service)

Denial of service attacks renders a computer network temporarily unresponsive. A hacker will intentionally create a server overload so that the server shuts down or slows to a crawl. This is a favorite tool used by "hacktivist" interested in making their protests known to the public. When we spoke earlier about CNN's network being slowed down for almost two hours, this was accomplished through a DoS.

John the Ripper (JTF)

Used in brute force password cracking to help hackers steal user passwords.

Keystroke Logging

The simplest explanation of keystroke logging is the creation of a map that shows the trails of computer and human interface. Hackers use keystroke logging to obtain login IDs and passwords.

Payload

Payload is the data being transmitted by a virus that destroys such data, harvests information, or hijacks your computer.

Packet Sniffer

No, it's not a working K-9, although they are programs designed to find and capture desired data. The term packet refers to the packages of information traveling through the Internet that typically contains the destination address and content. Once sniffed out, these packages can be used to steal login information and passwords.

Rootkit

A favorite of hackers, rootkits are a set of software programs that hackers use to access a system and set up malware. Rootkits enable hackers to travel inside without detection. You'll never be the wiser.

Script Kiddie

Hackers consider this to be an insult to their skills. It refers to those wannabes who employ prefab cracking tools to attack systems. Script Kiddies mistakenly think they will impress their peers; the real hackers can spot a script kiddie a mile away.

Spoofing

Spoofing is when email headers are altered or replaced, so they appear to come from somewhere else. For example, a hacker might change his header, so it looks like it was sent from your bank. IP spoofing is when a packet is forwarded to a computer with an altered IP to imitate a familiar host. In this way, the hacker hopes the packet will be accepted and then the hacker is in like Flynn.

Note: All glossary terms referenced by notes (38) (39).

Much like Maslow's Hierarchy of Needs, hackers also have a hierarchy of needs to make it possible for them to meet their goals. Their needs look something like this.

Basic Needs

Their first and most basic needs are just like the rest of us. They need shelter and food, but that's where the hierarchy begins to split. Where most of us need to feel safe, belong, experience love, and reach our potential, hackers seem to play by an entirely different set of rules. Although they need a place to live and work, they don't require it to be that nice. In fact, hackers are much more comfortable surrounded by cords, wires, motherboards, an entire network of computers, servers, and a very comfortable chair.

The seat is most important, since they spend many hours working from their chair, and most nights sleeping in it. Hackers feel about their chairs like most of us feel about our beds.

Money

Depending on the hacker's level, the funding required can be over the top of most people's electronics budget. Standard for most at home users is one computer—perhaps if you consider yourself techy, you'll have two screens or a docking station. You might have an external hard drive, a couple of speakers, and a printer. While the money to supply normal computer use can be expensive, it can't hold a candle to the high cost of providing a hacker with his or her tools of the trade.

Hackers would feel stripped if they didn't have more than a minimum of three computers, and preferably more. They need additional tools like solders, development boards, amplifiers, voltage regulators, microchips, cables, more memory, sefuse cutoffs, cameras, and some extra storage is always good. These would only be a starter's kit. At the risk of justifying their actions, the money needed to keep a hacker updated requires many of them to turn Black Hat.

One advantage, it's never a challenge decided what to get a hacker for birthdays or Christmas—more equipment.

Connectivity

Hackers must be connected to a network which allows them to reach their targets.

Target Vulnerabilities

Hackers need vulnerabilities and exposure to successfully exploit, practicing and honing their hacking skills so they can someday achieve their goal of zero-day discoveries.

Capabilities and Infrastructure

Moving higher up on the hacker's hierarchy of operational needs are capabilities and infrastructure. They need the capabilities to reach their desired effect, and the infrastructure to send those results to their targeted victims.

Targets

Hackers usually have many targets with much malware working on those targets at the same time. If hackers have no targets, then the challenge dies. They set a target to achieve their goals. Sounds almost like a young executive, don't you think. However, the goals of young executives are usually not to destroy or damage.

Access

To snoop, spy, locate vulnerabilities, damage, and destroy, hackers must gain access to your computer. No access—no hack!

Outcome

Even though most hackers like to fly by the seat of their pants, it's important for them to have the desired outcome planted in their heads of what they wish to achieve. Otherwise, the hacker is just roaming willy-nilly through computers with no path or direction. Hackers cannot realize success if they don't know their final destination expectations.

Reward

Hackers must be motivated like all of us—so, what's the payoff? What is it that the hacker wants to achieve? It could be fame, fortune, notoriety, destruction, or fun (40).

Oh, a little bit of knowledge in the hacker's world can get you in a whole lot of trouble. As curious as I know hackers to be, I can sometimes let my curiosity get the best of me as well. For example, after looking at all these tools of the trade that hackers use to work their dark magic, I began to wonder where they got what they needed for success. I don't know about you, but I haven't seen a strip center lately with a storefront that touted malware for sale. Come in today and buy a few stolen credit cards and some computer passwords.

Well, that's not how the "Dark Traders" work. Like every other part of their business, they rent, buy, sell, and trade products and services through the online black market. It's like a giant flea market for illegal goods and services. The most important requirement for dark traders is to use anonymous channels for their transactions—for obvious reasons. It's a virtual stock(ed) market, with prices that rise and fall according to demand.

There's no sales tax or charge fees, but the payment can be a bit tricky. A lot of Bitcoin is used, and then there's always the trade. If cash is needed, you can depend on the criminals to figure a way convenient payment plan through Western Union. A few years ago, dark traders attracted national attention when Target's security was breached. It was reported that hackers obtained 40 million credit cards and hijacked 70 million user accounts. Where did they find them? You got it—on the hackers' black market. Within days the black market was flooded with Target's goods (41).

So who's minding the stores in this black market? Cybercriminals, of course. The black market is a virtual flurry of business conducted between hackers. It includes offers for the production of malware, data sales, and any number of illegal cyber products taken from unsuspecting users.

Black Market Frequent Flyers

People who frequently shop on the black market sites are not just hackers, but all types of cyber criminals.

- Web Designers

  Providers of web designs create malicious sites that are so close to the real thing that users are fooled by their official looking logos and authoritative verbiage. One way users can tell if the website is malicious is to look for misspelled words and errors in sentence structure and grammar. Hackers may be great at design, but they haven't perfected the English language.

- Programmers

  Many of these programmers who are developing malware are so talented that corporate America would give their right arm to hire as well. It's a shame though that the hackers are making such advances in their craft that the security companies are finding it a challenge to keep up with the ever-growing talents of these programmers.

- Hackers

  A tremendous number of hackers offer all types of services and products on the black market. The hackers value is that they can exploit system vulnerabilities and break into computer networks. When this is achieved, they don't just get one or two items, but they have a field day with millions of people's personal, financial, or intellectual property.

- Tech Experts

  These are your maintenance people. It's the tech experts who offer their services to maintain servers and databases. It's a tidy criminal circle they operate.

- Intermediaries

  This includes a broad category of crooks who collect stolen data, promote and advertise it to other crooks in the black market, and sell or exchange their wares for money or more liquidatable items. Their job is often more challenging than most because it often requires trust between people who are not known to be trustworthy.

- Fraudsters

  These are the con artists who devise many of the phishing and spam schemes. Fraudsters also include many creative social engineering schemes that feature the latest and most effective ways to hook users like you and me.

Once the cybercriminals have hocked their wares, how are the payment exchanges made? Good question! It's not like they have a black market bank—or do they? In a sense, they do. Their computers are their banks. Their currency or commodities include credit card numbers, email addresses lists, access to hacked servers, and counterfeit currency, to name a few methods.

Here's how the process works. Black market vendors are contacted via underground forums or through social media. The dark traders conduct private chats or email one another using generic addresses, of course. From there they begin to negotiate their transactions. Some stores purchase products and services. Some stores sell illegal goods and services. And then some stores distribute the goods and services for other cyber criminals. It's a virtual hackers' mall.

Negotiations not only include the illegal properties and services, but they also negotiate how payment will be made. Prices may be raised or lowered depending on the method of payment. It's also possible to ask for customer support if you have purchased a product that is defective, and you wish to return it. For example, if a credit card is invalid, it can be exchanged for another.

When money is exchanged, it has to be laundered. This is where the money mules come into play. Cybercrooks create false job offers—I've often seen them on Craigslist or other job boards. The cyber crooks use their social engineering skills to entice those reading the ads to make inquiries. Of course, the victims are promised high commissions for simply receiving stolen money in their bank accounts and then sending it to foreign accounts via Western Union. Let this be a lesson to you if you are approached by someone and asked to accept Western Union transactions. It's a scam.

Years ago my friend answered an ad on Craigslist for a personal assistant. The job sounded perfect. She could work from home, spend more time with her kids, and it paid quite well. The "manager" told her he often traveled out of the country, and there would be money transferred via Western Union. He went on to say that there were no accounting services where he was traveling, so here's how they would handle her paycheck. Her first check would cover her pay for the week, and two weeks of company expenses while he was out of the country.

Her pay was $400 per week, and the additional two weeks' expenses equaling $1,000 would mean the check that would be delivered by mail to her home would be written for $1,400. When she received her check, she was to withdraw $1,000 from her bank account and send it via

Western Union to the address he would provide. Then she could go to the bank and deposit the check into her account once the accountant had notified her that he had received the cash.

What that meant to my friend, was that she was expected to withdraw $1,000 of her own money, send it via Western Union, and then wait to cash her $1,400 check until the cash was received. Meanwhile, it was her money on the line. Once she understood how payment was—or was not— to be made, she thought better of accepting the job as personal assistant.

Although the black market can be exciting to visit, it's wise to stay clear of these dark traders. Just entering the site may compromise your computer. You can bet all those who participate in the trades are checking out everyone who comes and goes on the site. You might become easy pickins' for the savvy traders. By paying a little more on legitimate sites, you could be saving yourself tons of money and aggravation in the long run. Leave the black market to the dark traders.

Another lesson to be learned here is to be very careful what job offerings you answer. Hackers and cyber criminals troll these boards and look for those who seem naïve and unaware. Shortly after responding to a job placement ad, you may find strange things going on with your computer. The red flags to look for go something like this.

- You'll never actually meet or speak to the person advertising the position.
- Anything involving Western Union is a dead giveaway that the ad is not on the up and up.
- Never take money from your account to send to someone that you don't know.
- The manager or your boss will almost always be out of the country, asking you to do things that involve exchanges of money from your account to his or hers.
- There is usually a friend or accountant to whom you'll have to send the cash—never the name on the posting.

Don't you wonder how truly successful hackers and cyber criminals would be if they used all their talent and creativity on legitimate endeavors? The schemes they devise are quite intricate. They are so convincing sometimes that I believe they could talk a dog into fleas. We all need to keep our wits about us as we travel the Internet.

The tools we have been given is common sense, intuition, and discernment. Even if you aren't as savvy as the hackers when it comes to computers, there's no need to be street stupid. Instead of hoping you don't run into cybercriminal on a job board like Craigslist, why not simply decide to stay clear of them? The crooks have hoodwinked so many people; it amazes me how common sense isn't so common these days.

Conclusion: Once Innocent—Now Hacked

The following stories are of people who experienced hackers first hand and lived to tell about it. Being victimized by a hacker is a sobering experience; once you've had it happen to you the thought of security software doesn't sound so expensive after all. Hopefully, you don't learn the hard way about lost data, stolen passwords, and emptied bank accounts like the people in these stories. Don't make the following stories to have been shared in vain. Learn from the stories these people have to tell, and decide not to join their ranks.

Held for Ransom

Alina's mother had a decision to make. Before this, she had never heard of ransomware, never realized that someone could send her an email that would encrypt everything on her computer, only promising to restore it when she paid the hacker's ransom. To be honest, she didn't even know what a hacker was. She had heard about computer systems being broken into, but she thought that was all government espionage stuff. It never happened to the little guy, right?

She knew she should be backing up her computer, but she never thought to do so until she had already shut down her machine. She was ashamed to admit it, but it had been six months since she had backed up her information. Alina's mother begrudgingly decided to pay the extortion fees, but the process was a lengthy, cumbersome, and quite a costly one.

Don't be like Alina's mother. Backup your information. CryptoWall infections are devastating to the user, and the emotional stress suffered because you failed to back up your files is what the hacker counts on to collect his ransom.

A New Kind of Hack—Carjacking

It was quite a reality check when Andy Greenberg, senior writer at Wired, decided to participate in a carjacking experiment. He agreed to let a hacker attempt to remotely control his car while he was behind the wheel. Once the public learned this could happen, we all began to live Andy's nightmare. The experiment with Andy's Jeep uncovered a major flaw in Jeep's vehicles, requiring a recall by the manufacturer to patch its software. The ramifications of this story are here to stay since this is just the beginning of a whole new hacking era attacking the computers in the cars on our roads.

Too Late to Learn

This desperate cry for help is all too familiar in today's forums. This university student had worked for two years to perfect his academic paper when he was attacked by a hacker using ransomware. All his work was encrypted, and the hacker's timing couldn't have been more opportune. The user attempted to recover his paper with an antivirus, but to no avail. Unfortunately, just like Alina's mom, this student had also failed to practice the proper security measures and back up his work.

When backup is so easy and flash drives or external hard drives so affordable, why take the chance? Protect your files. As any hacker worth his "salt" will tell you, you may not have your files around forever.

Game Gone Bad

Players who are heavy into their gaming have repeatedly been the target for hackers. Some have taken years to build their characters and enhance that character's skills, and recovery would be next to impossible. It can also be a significant expense if the gamer had to rebuild their reputation in their gaming universe.

This poor guy not only had his WoW account hacked, which resulted in the loss of all his progress but once was not enough for these hackers. He had it happen to him again. Never underestimate the creativity of a cyber criminal.

How Is the Government Handling Your Data?

Jonathan had just become a statistic in the latest OPM data breach. By mistake, of course, the government had handed over to a cyber criminal all of Jonathan's data. Within a short period of time, it went public. This was no "oops" issue, and the government hadn't intended for it to happen. However, that doesn't make Jonathan comfortable knowing that everybody and his brother now knows each minute detail of his life. Jonathan's exposed personal information included his weight, height, hair and eye color, citizenship status, name address, police record, and all his contact information as well.

There wasn't much Jonathan could do after the fact except what many of us should do. He put pressure on the authorities to step up their cyber security measures to protect the rights of its citizens.

A Match Made in Hell

Although this woman lost her information to a scam artist on Match.com, her emotional devastation was much worse. The hacker stole her heart, hopes, and expectations for a bright future. She finally had something or someone to believe in again; too bad it was a cyber criminal. What began as an online scam, permanently altered the dreams of a lonely woman who will most likely never trust again. There are ways to protect yourself from these hateful types of hackers, but you have to open your eyes to all the possibilities and refuse to be victimized. Even then it could happen, but your chances of an online hack decrease significantly when you educate and protect yourself by being in the know.

There Are No Do-overs

The minute she clicked the rogue link, Amanda knew she had made an irreversible mistake. Her work for a website company had educated her as to the importance of security, and Amanda had practiced some basic precautionary measures to protect her from cyber attacks. However, armed with all her knowledge and care, Amanda still fell for one the most common scams—a phishing email.

Once the email was opened, there was no going back—no do-overs. The hackers managed to empty £240 from her bank account before she could pick up the phone and freeze her cards. It was too late for Amanda; the hacker was faster than lightening striking a steel rod. Treat yourself to some much-needed online education, or read back through this book one more time to stay informed about what to do and what NOT to do.

Double Whammy

It's unimaginable, but Jason fell for the same "frequent flyer miles" scam twice in the same week. Really? Seems ridiculous, but it has happened to many before Jason. Unfortunately, Jason was unemployed at the time. In fact, he was about to take a trip before settling down to plan the next step in his career search. Isn't that always the time hackers take advantage, when you're down and out and need to take a few affordable shortcuts to achieve your dreams?

Knowing he needed to get away but his finances were limiting his desired destinations, Jason searched the Internet hoping to find a great deal. Wow, he couldn't believe his good fortune (and perhaps he shouldn't have believed it) when he came across this travel site that promised fares half the price of those he had previously seen advertised. He snatched them up immediately, eager to share his find with his girlfriend.

When she heard how fantastic the offer was, she wanted to join in the fun. So, Jason went back to the sight and booked another flight. Although he hadn't heard of this particular travel agency, the website looked professional—well, all except for a few misspelled words here and there.

Searching on an unknown website for a deal that was crazy reasonable, Jason lost $1,350. Not once, but twice Jason was taken advantage of by the hacker. It was a double whammy for both Jason and his (now ex) girlfriend.

The Call Nobody Wants to Get

When Tom answered his phone, not in a million years did he suspect he was about to become the latest victim of an expert social engineered hack. The formal sounding gentleman sounded so contrite as he apologized to Tom for the possible compromise of his bank account. He continued to inform Tom that they feared the worst, that his accounts had been hacked and he might be in danger of losing money if they couldn't verify where the money had gone. He asked Tom to verify his account information so they could quickly put alerts on the hacked accounts and see if any funds could be recovered.

Tom was so frightened and frustrated that he gave the gentleman his information in hopes his money wouldn't be lost. He was asked to hold while the bank official attempted to flag the bank's system to see what could be done. Tom waited, and waited, and waited. When one minute rolled into another, Tom began to suspect something else even more dastardly than the first report was happening.

While hanging on the line, he picked up his cell phone and called his bank. To his dismay, his suspicions came to pass. All the money in his account had just been removed. He had been

hacked by the best, and his accounts emptied—
fooled by the understanding voice of brutal
hacker (42).

When Work Isn't Working

Donna was busy at work when suddenly her
computer shut down—totally black. The first
thing she did was check all the plugins.
Everything looked okay there. Then she visited
her friend down the hall, and before she could
get to her office, they both met in the hall with
the same look of confusion plastered across their
faces. Donna's co-worker had experienced the
same thing.

The next thing they did was contact their IT
department. It was then that the panic set in.
They were used to seeing the IT guys all kicked
back in their chairs with their feet propped up,
contemplating the next computer software they
could develop to make everyone's jobs more
efficient. However, this was not the case that

day. The IT department was chaotic. They were almost paralyzed with confusion—like a deer in headlights.

Donna listened as the manager of IT told those showing up at his desk that there was a problem and they'd let them know when things were back to normal. Unfortunately, things didn't return to normal for quite some time, for Donna or her company. Not only had the business been hacked, but many of the employee files had been obtained by the cybercriminals—Donna's included.

Donna was unable to save the money in her bank accounts, she lost her identity, and for years to come, she was repeatedly audited by the IRS. She tried to get a loan to see her through, but with all her financial woes she couldn't qualify. She ended up losing her home, her car, her marriage, and her peace of mind. It is seven years after the attack, and Donna's life is just beginning to return to normal. Now she can start rebuilding her life all over again.

Don't let yourself be the next featured story in a book about hackers. It can't be stressed enough how important it is to protect your information, your files, and your emotional peace-of-mind. For some reason, people tend to think that what is placed privately into a computer will remain that way. Although it would be wonderful if that were the case, it's up to us to make sure we don't make foolish mistakes.

Some of us learn the hard way to watch our backs. If that's you, take another read through the book and see if something jumps out at you that you didn't catch before. Whatever you do, refuse to allow yourself to set the book down and forget about all the things you have learned. Instead of thinking you couldn't be hacked, act as if you are in danger right now of being hacked, and do whatever it takes to protect yourself. It could be true. It could be you.

You can no longer plead ignorance, and, besides, when it comes to being hacked ignorance isn't bliss. What you don't know can and will hurt you. There are also some of you who will be intrigued by what you have read—curious to know more about hackers. If that is the case, there is nothing there for you. Your curiosity could get you into a lot of trouble when it comes to hackers. They are not to be trusted. So, if you think you can move in and out of their world just for fun—you are fooling yourself.

If you have children who are young adults and they're spending a lot of time on the computer, do a little snooping. Make sure they aren't part of a subculture of people you know nothing about. If you look back on many of the hackers you learned about in this book; they started when they were quite young. Even if your children aren't toying with the idea of hacking, they could be victimized by a clever hacker when they're surfing the net.

It never hurts to share information with your children. Let them know what you've been reading about in this book. Open up a dialogue with them about stranger danger on social media and in email messages. Worse than having all your files stolen would be to have a cyber criminal hijack your teenager. So, let them know you are concerned about what you read and ask for their input and insight.

In most cases, hackers and cyber criminals come in when they are invited, unintentionally perhaps, but still the door is opened for them most of the time. Many don't have to break into your computer or phone; you allow your sites and accounts to be compromised because you don't see the hacker lurking until it's too late. A little bit of knowledge isn't dangerous; it's awakening. Be attentive to the subject lines in your emails. If you don't know the sender, don't open them. Look carefully at the sites you visit. If the grammar is poor and the spelling is that of an uneducated person, leave the site. If you are being led to another site with urgency or in a threatening manner, don't follow.

I just recently heard that today's hackers are so much different than yesterday's group who were, for the most part, out to see what they could prove and to raise a little trouble along the way. There's a new name for today's hackers. We've already talked about the Black Hat, White Hat, and Grey Hat hackers. Now we have Green Hat hackers. What does the green stand for—money.

Green Hat hackers are in it for the money. They don't care who they step on to get what they want. These Green Hat hackers are a combination of sophistication, greed, and heartlessness. That's an extremely dangerous mix. Get in their way, and you may find yourself sucked into one of their schemes. Cross them, and it's even worse. They treat hacking like a business, and nobody messes with their business. They aren't the geeks or the gearheads, and they aren't the script kiddies or the up and coming professionals. Green Hat hackers are strictly there to extort money from you—to rob and steal.

If you're worried about your child's behaviors that you believe may be a signal that he's getting into the world of hacking, look for the following.

- Is your child isolated with the computer when he or she is not in school?
- Does he rarely have friends over?
- Does he or she act superior when it comes to the computer, becoming frustrated and annoyed with your lack of knowledge?
- Does your child often eat at the computer?
- Does your child tend to be careless with his or her appearance, not wanting to take away from time that could be spent at the computer?
- Does your child hide what he or she is doing on the computer when you come into the room?
- Is your child introverted, an awkward communicator?
- Does your child seem to speak a computer language you don't understand?

- Does your child seem fascinated with talking about or bragging about the workings of a computer?

All these could be signs that your child is too close to the fire. Computers can be wonderful tools. However, they can also be dangerous weapons. Make up your mind that you're not going to allow the computer to become the parent.

It might sound strange, but I know many parents who have allowed their children to be babysat or parented by a computer. The child spends more time each day in front of the computer than communicating with his or her family members. Before you know it, the child's world becomes a virtual reality where people die in games and can be brought back to life. They learn to react instead of respond. Children can be subjected to many things at the hands (or keys) of a computer. They can be bullied, enticed, assaulted, and unfairly influenced by others sitting at their keyboards. It's not a fair playing field. Computers set up a fantasy world where people can appear to be exactly how they want to describe themselves. They don't have to learn communication skills or coping strategies when things get tough they can shut down.

While a little bit of virtual is okay, too much tends to confuse the lines between what is real and what is the computer. As an adult, you have a better handle on what is reasonable and what could be a hack or a scam. However, as a youth or young adult, your child may not have fully developed their social skills. Most of the time, computers don't help a lot in the area of improving social behaviors.

Everything in moderation is a good plan to follow. Computers are exciting and open up so much to us, but they are not the end all to everything. Going on a hike, riding a horse, fishing in a stream, playing football, riding bikes, are all exciting and fun to do as well. It takes some effort on everyone's part, though, to plan outdoor activities for the day. When your week of work is over, sometimes you're just too tired to make yourself join in some outdoor fun.

Let me ask you a question—when was the last time you did an outdoor activity with your family? If you can't remember, shut off the computer and get busy planning a weekend of fun. At first, it may seem like a lot of bother, but soon it will become your new norm. Make a deal with your teens that you'll do tradeoffs. For every hour they spend on the computer, they agree to spend even just 30 minutes in outdoor activities. Go to your greenbelt and throw a football. Take the dogs for a walk. Make it competitive—kids love a good bet.

If it's you that is too attached to the computer, take a second look at your kids. Are they clamoring for your attention? Do you come home from work, park yourself in front of the TV with your iPad and call it quality time with the kids? Isn't it time for some significant changes in your life? Good!

Make a decision to get away from your gadgets tonight and talk to your friends, girlfriend, spouse, or children. If you live alone, get out there and make some new friends. Newsflash! Your computer has no feelings for you. It does not feel your pain. It cannot share your joy when you get a raise at work. It's a cold, hard box that spits back what others put inside. It cannot think or reason, and it is not your friend. All of those things are waiting for you on the outside of your room or office. So—take a walk on the wild side of reality. Enjoy all the colors and textures of the "real" world!

References

1. Sweatman, Will (2016), *"The Dark Arts: Meet the LulzSec Hackers,"* (www.hackaday.com/2016/01/26/the-dark-arts-meet-the-lulzsec-hackers), Retrieved October 1, 2016.

2. Apendix B.A. Portrait of J. Random Hacker, *"Personality Characteristics,"* (www.catlo.org/jargon/html/personality.html), Retrieved October 1, 2016.

3. Taylor, Ben, *"Why Is There a 1 in 3 Chance You'll Get Hacked in 2016?"* (https://www.bestvpn.com/blog/43225/get-hacked-one-in-three), Retrieved October 5, 2016.

4. Palmer, Shelly (2014) *"Five Ways You'll Be Hacked Any Time,"* (https://www.themontserratreporter.com/five-ways-youll-be-hacked-any-time), Retrieved October 5, 2016.

5. (same as above)

6. Ohlheiser, Abby (2016), *"Leslie Jones Was the Victim of a Hack, Reportedly Exposing Private Documents and Nude Photos,"* (https://www.washingtonpost.com/news/the-intersect/wp/2016/08/24), Retrieved October 6, 2016.

7. Cameron, Dell (2016), *"The Leslie Jones Hackers, If Caught, Could Face More Than 30 Years,"* (www.dailydot.com/.../leslie-jones-hackers-cfaai-joy-leiderman-ice-investigation), Retrieved October 6, 2016.

8. Guthrie Weissman, Cale (2015), *"9 Things You Can Hire a Hacker To Do and How Much It Will (Generally) Cost,"* (www.businessinsider.com/9-things-you-can-hire-a-hacker-to-do-and ...), Retrieved October 6, 2016.

9. Grossman, Jeremiah (2012), *"Tips for Not Getting Hacked on the Web,"* (https://www.whitehatsec.com/blog/tips-for-not-getting-hacked-on-the-web), Retrieved October 6, 2016.

10. Khan, Faisal (2011), *"How Can I Get In Touch With Underground Hackers?"* (https://www.quora.com/how-can-I-get-in-touch-with-underground-hackers), Retrieved October 6, 2016.

11. Bernard, Doug (2015), *"Hackers Hide Malware in Plain Sight,"* (www.voanews.com/a/hackers-hiding...in-plain-sight/2913694.html), Retrieved October 7, 2016.

12. MyDigital Shield (2015), *"5 Ways Hackers Gain Access To Your Data,"* (www.mydigitalshield.com/5-ways-hackers-gain-access-data), Retrieved October 7, 2016.

13. Bell, Steve (2015), *"How Hackers Access Your Computer,"* (www.bullguard.com/blog/2015/.../how-hackers-access-your-computer.html), Retrieved October 7, 2016.

14. (same as above)

15. *"Malware Definition,"* (www.techterms.com), Retrieved October 8, 2016.

16. Encyclopedia Britannica, *"Computer Virus,"* (www.britannica.com), Retrieved October 8, 2016.

17. VIRUS-L/comp.virus Frequently Asked Questions (FAQ) v 2.00 (Question B3: What is a Trojan Horse?) (1995), Retrieved October 8, 2016.

18. McDowell, Mindi, *"Understanding Hidden Threats: Rootkits and Botnets,"* US-CERT, Retrieved October 8, 2016.

19. Edwards, John, *"Top Zombie, Trojan Horse and Bot Threats,"* IT Security, Retrieved October 8, 2016.

20. Casey, Henry T. (2015), *"Latest Adware Disables Antivirus Software, Tom's Guide,"* (www.yahoo.com), Retrieved October 8, 2016.

21. Wikipedia: *"Malware,"* (https://en.wikipedia.org/wiki/malware), Retrieved October 8, 2016.

22. Hacker Psychology, Network World, *"Understanding the 4 Emotions of Social Engineering,"* (www.networkworld.com/.../hacker.psychology-understanding-the-4-emotions-of-social-engineering), Retrieved October 10, 2016.

23. Hamblen, Matt (2016), *"So Your Company's Been Hacked: How To Handle the Aftermath,"* (www.computerworld.com/.../so-your-

company-s-been-hacked-how-to-handle-the-aftermath), Retrieved October 8, 2016.

24.   Starks, Tim (2016), *"Russian Hackers Trying to Influence U.S. Elections, Conclude Top Intel Democrats,"* (www.politico.com/story/2016/09/russian-hackers-influence-election-228543), Retrieved October 10, 2016.

25.   Bhattacharyya, Suman (2016), *"Cyberattacks Against the U.S. Government Up 1,300% Since 2006,"* (www.thefiscaltimes.com/.../cyberattacks-against-us-government-1300-percent-since-2006), Retrieved October 10, 2016.

26.   Sarrel, Matt, *"9 Resources to Stay Current on Security Threats,"* (www.esecurityplanet.com/malware), Retrieved October 10, 2016.

27.   Spad, Mary (2012), *"An Unexpected Conversation with a Hacker,"*

(www.codingpad.maryspad.com/2012/09/08/unexpected-conversation-with-a-hacker), Retrieved October 10, 2016.

28. Bisson, David (2015), *"Inside the Mind of a Former Black Hat Hacker,"* (www.tripwire.com/home/featuredarticles), Retrieved October 10, 2016.

29. Shinder, Deb (2010), *"Hiring Hackers: The Good, the Bad and The Ugly,"* (www.techrepublic.com/.../hiring-hackers-the-good-the-bad-and-the-ugly), Retrieved October 11, 2016.

30. Hill, Kashmir (2015), *"Hundreds of People Who Want to Hire Hackers Just Got Outed,"* (www.fusion.net/story/138602/hundreds-of-people-who-want-to-hire-hackers-just-got-outed), Retrieved October 11, 2016.

31.   Wikipedia: *"George Hotz,"*
(https://en.wikipedia.org/wiki/george_H
otz), Retrieved October 11, 2016.

32.   Kumparak, Greg (2011), *"Apple Hires the
Guy Who Hacked Together a Better iOS
Notifications System,"*
(https://techcrunch.com/.../apple-hires-
the-guy-who-hacked-together-a-better),
Retrieved October 11, 2016.

33.   Wikipedia: *"Jeff Moss (hacker),"*
(https://en.wikipedia.org/wiki/Jeff_Moss
_(hacker), Retrieved October 11, 2016.

34.   Carlson, Nicholas (2011), *"How I Attacked
Facebook with a Virus and Got a Job—At
Facebook,"* (www.gizmodo.com/.../how-
hacking-facebook-got-this-man-hired-by-
facebook), Retrieved October 11, 2016.

35.   Yin, Sara (2011), *"7 Hackers Who Got
Legit Jobs From Their Exploits,"*
(www.pcmag.com/reviews/software/secu

rity/PCmagazine), Retrieved October 11, 2016.

36.   (same as above)

37.   PC Security (2013), *"Inside the Mind of a Famous Hacker,"* (https://www.zonealarm.com/blog/2013/08/inside-the-mind-of-a-famous-hacker), Retrieved October 11, 2016.

38.   Hopkins, Curt (2013), *"The Definitive Glossary of Hacking Termanology,"* (www.dailydot.com/debug/hacking-security-glossary-adware-bot-doxing), Retrieved October 12, 2016.

39.   Dalziel, Henry (2015), *"The Top Five Hacker Tools of 2015,"* (www.scitechconnect.elsevier.com/the-top-five-hacker-tools-of-2015), Retrieved October 12, 2016.

40.   Caltagirone, Sergio (2012), *"A Hacker's Hierarchy of Needs,"* (www.activeresponse.org/a-hackers-

heirarchy-of-needs), Retrieved October
12, 2016.

41. Contini, Alessandro, *"A Quick Tour in the
     Black Markets, the Places on the Web
     Where It Is Possible to Acquire or Rent
     Malicious Services and Illegal Products,"*
     (www.securityaffairs.com/wordpress/376
     25/cyber-crime/hackers-black-
     market.html), Retrieved October 12,
     2016.

42. Zaharia, Andra, *"12 True Stories that Will
     Make You Care About Cyber Security,"*
     (https://heimdalsecurity.com/blog/autho
     r/andra/), Retrieved October 12, 2016.

www.ingramcontent.com/pod-product-compliance
Lightning Source LLC
LaVergne TN
LVHW022306060326
832902LV00020B/3302